A Cornish Chronicle

SIR ALEXANDER
CAREW

A
CORNISH CHRONICLE

The Carews of Antony from Armada to Civil War

by

F. E. HALLIDAY

DAVID & CHARLES: NEWTON ABBOT

Printed in Great Britain by
Latimer Trend & Co. Ltd, Plymouth
for David & Charles (Publishers) Ltd
South Devon House Newton Abbot Devon

To
DAVID LEWIS

Contents

	PREFACE	*page* 11
1.	RICHARD CAREW THE ELDER	15
2.	CAREW AND QUEEN ELIZABETH	23
3.	RICHARD CAREW THE YOUNGER	34
4.	BRIDGET CHUDLEIGH	46
5.	THE WIDOWER	72
6.	REMARRIAGE	96
7.	REFLECTIONS	105
8.	THE FATEFUL THIRTIES	123
9.	THE BARONET	133
10.	ALEXANDER	144
11.	JOHN	156
	APPENDIX I: The Carews of Antony and the Edgcumbes	165
	APPENDIX II: Carew Relationships through the Chudleighs	166
	BIBLIOGRAPHY	167
	INDEX	169

7

List of Illustrations

Sir Alexander Carew
from the oil painting at Antony House   *frontispiece*
(photo: Charles Woolf)

MAP

South East Cornwall   14

Preface

This book is a sequel to my *Richard Carew of Antony* (1953), the story of three generations of the Carew family, from the Armada to the Civil War and Restoration, made possible by the discovery of information about Carew's son, another Richard, hitherto virtually unknown, and often confused with his famous father. I have also been able to add new material to my original study.

In the muniment room of Antony House, near Torpoint, are two manuscript books by the second Richard Carew, who became the first baronet shortly before his death in 1643. Of the first of these there are three copies:

1. The original of 207 pages written by Carew himself. It retains its original parchment binding on which there is much scribbling, apparently by Nicholas Kendall, rector of the neighbouring parish of Sheviock towards the end of the seventeenth century, and husband of Jane, daughter of Thomas Carew of Harrabeare. Kendall seems to have been responsible for the inscription: 'The Booke of M^{as} Richard Carew his one writtin hand. In the yeare of Lord God 1610.' The date is inaccurate, for the book was almost certainly begun in 1628 and finished in 1630.

2. A seventeenth-century transcript in a different hand, with an index or analysis of the contents.

3. A transcript dated 1802. The flyleaf has the note: 'This Book contains the Reflections of Sir Richard Carew B^n Son and Heire of Richard Carew, Author of the Survey of Cornwall. This Copy is in the Handwriting of Mr Tom, for many years

Steward in the family. The original was written in the year 1610, as appears by a Note thereon written by Sir Richard himself & now before me. Reginald Pole Carew. Antony June 9, 1802.'

The second manuscript book, of 56 leaves, was written in 1637. It is in the hand of the first transcriber of the 'Reflections', and headed, 'Sir Richard Carewes Booke presented by him to Mrs Buller.'

Sir Richard was much concerned with his own spiritual and physical wellbeing, but his great ambition was to do good to others, and his first book is primarily a passport to salvation, his second a guide to health and longevity. Much of the matter, however, is autobiographical, and as Elizabethan and Jacobean autobiographies are by no means common, it is this material that I have selected and arranged to form a continuous narrative, leaving Richard, as far as possible, to tell it in his own words. In addition to the story of his life, his hobbies, travels and adventures, there are anecdotes of witches and conjurers, including one about Dr Burcot and Queen Elizabeth, accounts of his humble neighbours and distinguished friends and relations, and reminiscences of his famous father. For Richard, the eccentric squire, is not only interesting in himself, he is also the link between the distinguished Elizabethan writer and the two sons who were to play their parts in the great drama of the Civil War and to suffer the same, though so different, fate. It is improbable that there were any other brothers, like Alexander and John, who were executed by the opposing parties of the struggle, the one by Parliament, the other by the Royalists. This chronicle of three generations, therefore, has a unity and completeness that are uncommon in history, in real life, and give it something of the quality of a novel, a dramatic structure with beginning, middle and end, the middle being supplied by this new information about the hitherto virtually unknown second Richard, who must be held partly responsible for the tragedy.

For the 'Duchy Suit' I am indebted to the Rev C. R. S. Enys, owner of the manuscript, to Mr P. L. Hull, the County Archivist, who edited the text with an introduction and notes, and to the Royal Institution of Cornwall in whose Journal it was published in 1962. I am also indebted to Professor G. H. Turnbull and his book, *Hartlib, Dury and Comenius*, for information about Carew's relations with Samuel Hartlib, and to Lord Delamere for permission to quote from Hartlib's papers; to Mr Charles Thomas for lending me what is apparently Carew's own annotated copy of his *Survey of Cornwall*; and to Sir John Carew Pole of Antony, without whose generous help this book could not have been written.

F. E. HALLIDAY

St Ives
Cornwall

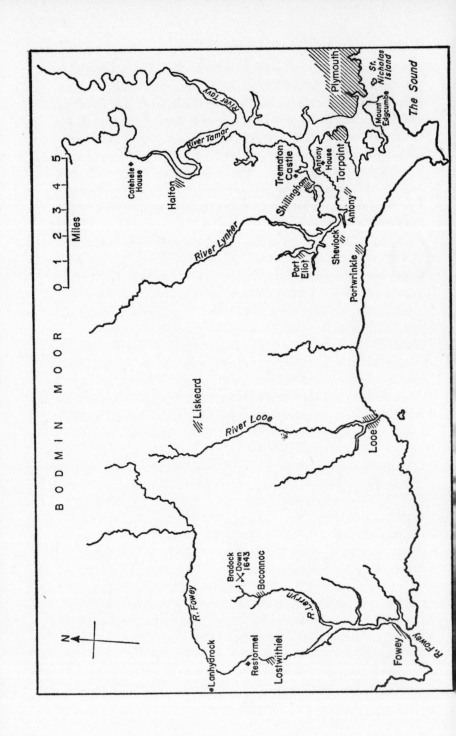

Richard Carew the Elder

One of the most delectable—and inaccessible—regions of Cornwall is the country defined on the north by the upper waters of the Fowey where it cuts across the southern slopes of Bodmin Moor, on the west by its lower reaches as it turns abruptly at Lanhydrock and slides below the Black Prince's castle of Restormel into its long tidal estuary, on the east by the Looe River, and on the south by the sea. It is virtually an island carved out of the country by rivers, the kingdom of Mark and Isolde and magical Celtic names, approximately the old Hundred of West, forming an almost perfect square, its sides eight miles long, with the little towns of Fowey, Lostwithiel, Liskeard and Looe at the four corners. Near the middle of this square is Boconnoc.

The house was rebuilt and the grounds laid out in the eighteenth century, and little remains of the medieval house in which, at the time of the Wars of the Roses, lived Sir Hugh Courtenay, son of the Earl of Devon. Sir Hugh, a staunch Lancastrian, was executed after the Yorkist victory at Tewkesbury in 1471, leaving his wife Philippa and an only daughter Joan, who inherited her mother's estate. Joan married twice and outlived both her husbands, her first one being Sir Nicholas Carew of Haccombe in Devon, a member of the ancient family of Montgomery in south Wales, who had changed their name after their acquisition of Carew Castle, near Pembroke. Joan had five sons by Sir Nicholas, with the eldest of whom, Thomas, she quarrelled, an event that was to be described by her Elizabethan descendant a century later: 'which discord (with an unnatural extremity) brake forth into a blow, by him no less dearly than undutifully given his mother; for upon so just a cause she disinherited him of all her lands, being seventeen manors, and bestowed them on her younger sons.' In this way her fourth son, Alexander, inherited the manor of Antony in Cornwall.

Like Boconnoc, Antony House was rebuilt in the eighteenth century. It stands on the peninsula formed by the confluence of the rivers Lynher and Tamar, between the village of Antony and Torpoint, its wooded grounds sloping down to the tidal Lynher, on the other side of which is Shillingham, former home of the Bullers, the ruined keep of Trematon Castle and a distant prospect of the northern hills. Here, in the original house, in the middle of the sixteenth century lived Alexander's great-grandson, Thomas Carew, a young man of twenty-three, who had inherited the estate on the death of his father in 1549.

A few miles farther up the Tamar, on its precipitous western bank, was Cotehele, the home of Sir Richard Edgcumbe, the finest medieval house in Cornwall, with fifteenth-century courtyard, chapel and great hall. It was the work principally of his father and grandfather, but Sir Richard hankered after something more compact and convenient in the latest Tudor style, and was at this time building a remarkably up-to-date house on another peninsula south of Antony, overlooking Plymouth, the Sound and the fortified outpost of St Nicholas Island. Mount Edgcumbe was 'builded square, with a round turret at each end, garretted on the top, and the hall rising in the midst above the rest, which yieldeth a stately sound as you enter the same'. It was, perhaps, the first house in the country to have a central hall lighted by a clerestory. No wonder the commander of the Spanish Armada thirty years later coveted this high-seated house by the sea.

Young Thomas Carew would welcome the move of the Edgcumbes from Cotehele to Mount Edgcumbe, for Sir Richard had a daughter, Elizabeth, and shortly after the accession of Queen Mary he carried her back to Antony as his wife. Their happiness lasted only a decade, however, for in 1564, the sixth year of Queen Elizabeth's reign and the year of Shakespeare's birth, Thomas died, leaving his widow with three young children, Richard, George and Elizabeth.

Thus Richard Carew, born in 1555, found himself lord of the manor of Antony at the age of nine, a circumstance that he ever regretted, for the care of his estates prevented his travelling abroad and learning the languages—French, German, Spanish, Italian—which he had so laboriously to teach himself.

When he was only eleven he went to Oxford as a gentleman-commoner of Christ Church, with rooms in Broadgates Hall. His slightly older contemporary at Christ Church was Philip Sidney, with whom, when he was only fourteen, he was 'called to dispute *extempore* in presence of the Earls Leicester, Warwick and divers other great personages'. His distinguished and adventurous kinsman, Sir Peter Carew, a descendant of the disinherited Thomas, was also there, and assured him that he need not be disconcerted by Sidney's grand relations, for was not he, Richard Carew, descended from Welsh princes, and even, though perhaps a little obliquely, from the Conqueror himself? Which was more than these upstart Dudleys could boast. This enforced and formal disputation only confirmed the friendship of the two boys, and Sidney always remained for Carew 'the miracle of the age', and no doubt inspired his passion for writing.

In 1574 he left Oxford and entered the Middle Temple to learn something about law and the management of his estates. Two years later he came of age, and in the following January rode across to Bokelly, near Wadebridge, to hawk with 'old William Carnsew' and his friends, and perhaps with one or more of his three sons, Richard, Matthew and William, Oxford men like himself. A few days later he appears to have ridden westward again, through Wadebridge to Trerice, near Newquay, to stay with John Arundell, for on the 21 January Carnsew met them both at a neighbouring house.

The Arundells were the wealthiest and most powerful family in Cornwall, and in 1577 John Arundell was a happy man. He had recently completed the rebuilding of Trerice, more conservative than Mount Edgcumbe, with scrolled gables in the

Dutch manner, a slpendid hall lit by a huge mullioned window, a minstrel gallery and fine plaster ceilings; and in the previous year his wife had presented him with his first son, another John, for all the eldest Arundell boys were Johns. He already had four daughters, two of them by his first wife, Catherine Coswarth, and one of these, Juliana, was the real object of Richard's January pilgrimage. A few months later they were married, and Juliana Arundell, a girl of fourteen, succeeded Elizabeth Edgcumbe as mistress of Antony.

They had ten children, the first born in 1579, the last in 1604, three of them dying in infancy, and only five, all boys, survived their father. John, the eldest, was the first to go, but in 1580 a second son, another Richard, was born, not at Antony however, but at his mother's home, Trerice. Perhaps Juliana had gone to attend her father's funeral, for John Arundell died that year, and his four-year-old son John became head of the family.

Young John's nephew, the second Richard Carew, was born at the beginning of the most stirring decade in our history. In 1580 Drake sailed into Plymouth after an absence of three years, during which, 'as an emulator of the sun's glory he had encompassed the world'. The phrase is Carew's, who saw his return. His friend Philip Sidney was writing his sonnets and *Arcadia*, and fighting the Spaniards in the Netherlands, where he was mortally wounded, 'One whom England sole did since the Conquest breed.' The twenty years' war with Spain had begun, and in 1588 the great Armada that was to have carried an army into England was foiled by Drake and destroyed by storms. Spenser was publishing his first poetry, and young Christopher Marlowe from Cambridge and William Shakespeare from Stratford arrived in London to revolutionize the drama.

They were also stirring years for Carew. In 1581 he was appointed a justice of the peace, one of those responsible for the local government of Cornwall, for in Tudor times justices *were* the local government. Soon he was sheriff and a member of Parliament, and one of the deputy-lieutenants charged with the defence of the county, in which office he saw the English fleet beat out of Plymouth Sound to engage what he called 'the

Spanish floating Babel' as it passed Mount Edgcumbe, where one great galleon was crippled.

He can have had little leisure during these memorable years, and he satisfied his passion for learning by reading as he rode from Antony to the sessions at Bodmin and Truro, and even as he walked down to fish in the saltwater pond that he had made on the shore of the Lynher. And on his journeys he was constantly collecting material for the description of Cornwall that his Oxford friend, William Camden, in his *Britannia* of 1586, assured his readers that he was writing: 'Sed haec planius et plenius docebit Richardus Carew de Anthonie, non minus generis splendore, quam virtute et doctrina nobilis, qui hujus regionis descriptionem latiore specie, et non ad tenue, elimat.' ('But Richard Carew of Antony will explain these things more plainly and fully, a man no less distinguished by his parentage than by his own virtue and learning, who is writing a full description of this county.')

The defeat of the Armada and recession of the danger of invasion gave him a little more time. His brother George, a rising diplomat in London, had married the daughter of Sir Francis Godolphin, who lived in the far west of the county, where he employed some three hundred people in his tin mines, and it was on a visit to Godolphin Hall that Carew picked up a book that interested him. This was an Italian version of the *Examen de Ingenios para las Ciencias* by the Spanish physician Juan Huarte. As Carew had taught himself both Spanish and Italian, and the scientific study of men's minds was the kind of subject that aroused his curiosity, he borrowed the book and, neglecting his 'Description of Cornwall', spent his spare time translating it. It appeared in the summer of 1590 as *The Examination of Men's Wits,** with a charming dedication to Godolphin:

> Good Sir, your Booke returneth unto you clad in a Cornish gabardine, which if it become him not wel, the fault is not in the stuffe, but in the botching Tailor, who never bound Prentice to

---

* In my *Richard Carew of Antony* I wrote that the book was first published in 1594. Mr John Crow points out that there is a copy of a very rare 1590 edition at Harvard.

the occupation, and working only for his passe-time, could hardly observe the precise rules of measure: but such as it is, yours it is and yours is the workeman . . . R.C.

Huarte's book is important as the first—and often fantastic— attempt to demonstrate the relationship between physiology and psychology, so that every man, to his great advantage, can find the work to which he is by nature best adapted. For, Huarte argues, there is an art to find the mind's construction in the face, or at least in the body and certain observable characteristics. Thus, a moist constitution betokens a good memory, a bald head imagination, and poor hand-writing intelligence. As climate is partly responsible for physical characteristics, so is it for the quality of mind; the Mediterranean, for example, produced the perfectly tempered Jesus of Nazareth, an auburn haired man of medium height, a man indeed, when you come to think of it, not unlike Philip II of Spain, to whom Huarte had dedicated his book. As the drift of his argument became apparent to the protestant Carew, he enlivened the text with marginal growls: 'Take heed you receive no hurt for leaving out the Pope.' 'And such a one if you mistake not is your king Philip.' Finally, when Huarte observes that 'nature shapeth so few after this model that I could never find but two among all the wits that I have tried,' the exasperated Carew remarks tartly, 'Your king and your self.'

The Examination of Men's Wits was an immediate success; the first edition was soon exhausted, another appeared in 1594, and there were three more impressions in the next twenty years. This was partly because of the interest of the subject matter, which had given Huarte's book a European reputation, partly because of Carew's attractive and very readable translation. Although he modestly professed to write 'only for his passe-time', his prose is that of a born writer, an easy, companionable prose, as lively as it is various, ranging from such delicate phrasing as, 'These never take pleasure in the plains, but ever delight to walk alone thorough dangerous and high places, and to approach near steep down-falls,' to the humorous, 'Good practitioners do all piddle somewhat in the art of versifying.'

Perhaps he was referring diffidently to himself as one of these piddling versifiers, for another venture in the art of translation was his rendering of Tasso's romantic epic of the First Crusade, *Gerusalemme Liberata*. In some way, however, his manuscript got into the hands of a not over-scrupulous stationer, Christopher Hunt of Exeter, for whom part of the 1594 edition of *The Examination of Men's Wits* had been printed. Hunt sent it to a London printer, and early in 1594 published the first five cantos as: 'Godfrey of Bulloigne, or the Recoverie of Hierusalem. An Heroicall Poeme, written in Italian by Seig. Torquato Tasso, and Translated into English by R. C. Esquire.' Hunt wrote a prefatory Epistle to the Reader:

> It was my good hap of late to get into my hands an English translation of Seg. Tasso's *Jerusalem*, done (as I was informed) by a gentleman of good sort and quality, and many ways commended unto me for a work of singular worth and excellency: . . . whereupon I determined to send it to the press, wherein if my forwardness have forerun the gentleman's good liking, yet let me win you to make me happy with the sweet possession of your favours . . .

In those days an author had no redress against a stationer who published a work that had, in whatever way, come into his possession, and it may be that Hunt was responsible for the piratical issue of Shakespeare's *Love's Labour's Won*, for a few years later he had a copy of this unknown play in his stock. Carew was not unnaturally angry at this 'untimely birth' of his poem, for apart from the impudence, it was, as Hunt implies, incompletely revised; but all he could do was to prevent publication of the remaining cantos 'till the summer'. They were never published, perhaps because Carew was too busy with public affairs and his final revision of the *Survey*, and then by 1600 Edward Fairfax had published his famous translation of the poem.

Although Fairfax wrote with Carew's work in front of him, occasionally helping himself to a word or phrase, the two versions bear little resemblance to one another. Carew honestly tried to make his translation as literal as possible, but Fairfax freely paraphrased and elaborated, and out of the original created another work of art. Carew's verse, therefore, is often awkward and crabbed owing to his struggle to force each line of the Italian into a corresponding line of English, but at his best he writes with a simplicity that is beyond the art of Fairfax, and very close to Tasso:

> Ma nella bocca, ond' esce aura amorosa,
> Sola rossegia e semplice la rosa.

> But in her mouth, whence breath of love outgoes,
> Ruddy alone and single blooms the rose.

This is transformed by Fairfax into a conventional conceit:

> Her lips, where blooms nought but the single rose,
> Still blush, for still they kiss while still they close.

And the vigour of some of Carew's lines make Fairfax's elaborations sound commonplace and dull:

> And moist with blood, and full of death his face.

> The signs of death upon his face appear,
> With dust and blood his locks were loathly dight.

Fairfax is the more even and accomplished poet, but there are better things in *Godfrey of Bulloigne*.

2

Carew and Queen Elizabeth

The summer of 1594 was cold and wet, a miserable season following a long period of severe plague, when, after being closed for nearly two years, the London playhouses reopened, and the thirty-year-old Shakespeare and his company, Lord Chamberlain Hunsdon's, moved into Burbage's Theatre. Had Carew known it, and nobody would have appreciated the knowledge more, the greatest period in English literature was just beginning.

There was, however, much to occupy him during this time, besides his dispute with Christopher Hunt. 'A gent named Henry Megges', a 'foreigner' from the Isle of Ely, one Champneys, and one Edwards, had made a breach in the customary form of tenure on some of the ancient manors composing the Duchy of Cornwall, which belonged to the Crown, by securing leases from the Exchequer, and at the Lent Assizes at Saltash this new procedure was upheld. Carew, as a justice, was present, and realizing that this ruling might mean the general subversion of the old custom, involving higher rents and evictions, appealed to the Judge, Lord Anderson, who replied that his business was to deliver the law, and that the best course was for the tenants to appeal to Queen Elizabeth. A meeting of representatives from the Duchy manors was called, and Carew and his friend Jonathan Trelawny were elected leaders of a deputation who were to go to London to get a revocation of the new leases and a confirmation of the customary form of tenure.

Carew kept a record of the proceedings, a copy of which he later sent to Trelawny, and it was almost certainly he who wrote the numerous letters involved. Before the April Sessions at Bodmin he drafted a petition to the Queen, and letters to the most influential members of the Government and others most able to help them. On 18 April these were read and signed by the justices assembled at Bodmin. The letter to Lord Keeper Puckering summarizes their complaint:

> This poore sheire of Cornwall, wherein wee liue, is at this present many wayes distressed; by the inimies surprising our shipps; by fear of their invasions; by stopping of our accustomed trades; by dearth of victualls; by decay of the mines, and by the late infeccion of the plague; whereunto is adioyned another more harmfull plague of such as seeke to reape a priuate profitt with the undoing of a greate multitude. This . . . is now sought by ouerthrowinge in some perticular tenements the generall custome of the Duchie. . .

The letter to William Killigrew, a Cornishman and Groom of the Privy Chamber, is more picturesque in its detail:

> And which if it be now ouerthrowne in this happy tyme of her Heighnes raigne; as it would breed little benefitt unto her Ma: tie, soe would it thrust aboue 10,000 her Heighnes loyall subiects and poor tenauntes into extreame misery and beggerye, and only a few couetous caterpillars should suck the sweete sapp both from her Ma:tie and them.

There were similar letters to Lord Treasurer Burghley, Sir John Fortescue, Chancellor of the Exchequer, Lord Chief Justice Anderson, Sir Walter Raleigh, Lord Warden of the Stannaries, and to Raleigh's rival, the Queen's new favourite, the young Earl of Essex, a spoiled Adonis of twenty-eight, who was soon to raise a rebellion 'to rescue the Queen from her ministers', and perish on the block.

It was agreed that the deputies should start for London at the end of the month, meeting at Exeter for dinner on 30 April. That night they got as far as Honiton, and on the following day, reached Sherborne, whose Castle the Queen had acquired for Raleigh a few years before. But her former favourite was now in disgrace. She had recently discovered that he had committed the unpardonable offence of seducing and secretly marrying one of her Maids of Honour, Elizabeth Throckmorton, and for a time both were confined in the Tower. Raleigh appealed to the Queen for pardon, but though he was released from prison, he had to retire from Court to his estate at Sherborne. Carew, writing in the third person, describes their visit to the great man, a distant relation of his, now sulking and suspicious in his enforced retirement, distrusting the motives of any visitors.

'From Honiton they pitched next at Sherborne, and made repaire to Sir Walter Rawleigh . . . where they weare enter-tayned for some houres by Mr Adrian Gilbert, his halfe-brother, with viewing the newe buildings, and had their acesse delayd upon pretence of his sicknes (but more indeede through a conceite grounded upon a fore reporte that they ment either not to visitt him at all, or else only to doe it for a fashion sake, and not in any sort to rely upon his furtherance). Att last, as they grewe amongst themselues into termes of departure, ad-mittance was giuen. Whom they found lying upon a pallett in his little chamber; received a courteous welcome, and deliuered their letters. Which, after he had read, he alledged his indis-position of health and gave his aduise what course was fittest to be taken in following the suite (viz): not ouer many to shewe themselues therein . . . but principally to sollicite the Lord Treasurer. . . And though his lordship should at first oppose himselfe with sharp termes, yet weare they not to take dis-couragement, but to persist in their suite. . .

'Then the deputes told him what sinister report they heard was made of them and, with protestacion of the untruth it carried, besought his lordship not to creditt the same. They withall acknowledged how much in former occasions he had from tyme to tyme frended their country, and that this properly belonging to his office as heigh steward of the Duchie, they ought both first to seeke him, and ment principally to relye upon him. He made a sleight answeare, that he had not bene so enformed. And with witness of his former willingnes to pleasure the country, he promised now also to write in their behalfe. . .'

Thus, with flattery and protestation, the deputies allayed the suspicions of the former Captain of the Guard that they had called on him only in pity as the fallen favourite, convincing him, who was so eager to be convinced, that they valued his support more than that of any other (though they did not tell him of their letter to Essex) and left Sherborne with his letters to Fortescue, Burghley, his son Sir Robert Cecil, and his secretary, Mr Maynard.

They stayed at Salisbury and Staines, and reached London on Saturday 4 May. The next morning they called on Lord Anderson, who promised, 'I will doe you any good I can,' though he refused to appeal to the Queen on their behalf. Sir Henry Killigrew, William's elder brother, was more encouraging and helpful.

The Court was at Greenwich Palace, where, a few months later, Shakespeare was to make his first recorded appearance as an actor, and on Monday the deputies made their way down the river. There they found William Killigrew, to whom they delivered the letter from the justices and another from Sir Francis Godolphin, which was 'soe earnestly and effectually penned, and caryed such creditt in reguard of the writer, as by Mr Kelligrewe shewing them to her Ma: ^{tie} and the Lord Treasurer, the suite receiued noe slender furtherance.' No praise could be too high for Killigrew's courtesy and helpfulness, and Carew pays him a characteristic tribute, to be repeated later in the *Survey*: 'As he made his countrymen beholden to him beyond abillity or possibility of requitall, soe he gaue noe lesse reputacion to his country (in that it bred a gent of soe rare a kindness, honesty, and reputacion).'

Killigrew took the deputes to see Burghley, who told them to come again the next day and bring a written statement of the reasons on which their suit was grounded, but they had to spend two days searching the records and getting copies of the leases granted to Champneys and Edwards. Burghley, annoyed at the delay, said that they would have to wait until he had consulted the officers of the Exchequer, and when they met again he told them that 'noe custome could bee alledged by the tenauntes to barr the Queene from making her best profitt thereof.' To this 'they humbly answeared . . . that during the space of 260 yeeres the tenauntes and their aunscestors under her Ma: ^{tie} and her progenitors quietly enioyed their holdinges by such rents and fines as they now paid, and neuer any of them upon any occasion weare expulsed. . . And lastly . . . they chose rather to appeale unto her Heighnes clemencye, then to stand upon termes of lawe.'

Burghley, as the Queen's Treasurer with a Spanish war on his hands, was naturally anxious that the Duchy officials should extract the maximum rents from the royal Cornish estates, and the deputies found 'their suite at a stopp'. Killigrew, however, supported their suggestion of a direct appeal to the Queen, whom he had already informed of the suit, and she 'was gra-ciouslye contented to admitt the suitors to her royall presence, but disliked (as did all the other greatest and wisest personages) that so many came upp aboute it, and forbade their trouping togeather.'

Before seeing the Queen, however, the deputies very wisely decided to deliver the justices' letter to Essex, being careful to explain, of course, why they had thought it best not to ap-proach him at once. 'Mr Kelligrewe (untired though still busied in their causes) brought them on Whitsoun Eave into the Lobby; where, with excuse of soe long detayninge, they de-liuered the letter to his lordship, which, hauing perused, he very honourably and familiarly told them that, though he altogeather forbeare to intermeddle with finance as noe way appertaininge unto him, but unto others, yet in this case he would force his disposicion and bestowe his best trauaile to doe even more than he could, and thearefore required a sight of their reasons whereon their suite was grounded.' They told him that they had already given the Lord Treasurer their reasons, but as there was no love lost between the old minister and the young favourite, Essex 'replyed nothing, but that they should bring *him* their reasons'.

There follows a fascinating glimpse of Court life in this cold summer of intrigue, when Essex was competing for power with the aged Burghley and his hunchback son, Sir Robert Cecil, who was being groomed to fill his father's place. The Lord Admiral, Lord Howard of Effingham, who had commanded the fleet against the Armada, one of the most attractive characters of the age, was above all such intrigue, though he was soon to be involved in a battle of wits with Essex.

'On Whitsunday in the morning all the deputes resorted to the Court, where, after they had sought my Lord of Essex att his lodginge in vaine (who was before gone upp by a priuye way to the Queene), they by greate chance not long after mett his lordship going alone to the Chappell and tooke that oppertunitye of deliuering their reasons, which weare in effect all one with the former. His lordship read them whiles hee satt at service, and so retourned.' It is a revealing picture, this, of Essex reading his mail at prayers.

'Mr Kelligrewe guided the deputes to the place where they should stand for deliuery of their peticion, being on the right side of the Chapple dore, and by good happ their countryman Goite, one of the guarde, wayted that day and kept them from thrusting. A little before her Ma: ᵗⁱᵉ came foorth, Mr Kelligrewe placed himselfe amongst them, and as her Heighnes approached, the Earle of Essex (who supported her on the one side as my Lord Admirall did on the other) moued her Ma: ᵗⁱᵉ in their behalfe. Whereon her Heigness comming neere them asked which weare they. Who therewith on their knees deliuered their peticion, hauinge that of the justices inclosed, and besought her Ma: ᵗⁱᵉ to stand gratious to her poore tenauntes of the Duchie of Cornwall. Her Heighnes, so neere as could be remembered, spake as followeth. "There are many foolish things gotten out against, but it shalbe remedied, and I would they weare hanged who haue bene the doers hereof, for wee respect the publique more than the priuate." Hereon the deputes with one voice gaue most humble thankes, and besought God long to preserue her Ma: ᵗⁱᵉ. The Earle of Essex, comming out againe shortly after, told them that they weare nowe in a good way.'

The Queen gave the petitions to the Countess of Warwick, widow of another favourite, and she spoke kindly to the deputies when they called on her, for she said she respected Cornishmen, 'for that the Earle her father had borne greate affeccion to those westerne parts and receiued like love from them againe.' Her father, Lord Russell, had good reason to feel affection for Cornishmen, for he had crushed their rebellion against the new Prayer Book in 1549, hanging his captives, and receiving the Earldom of Bedford and the manor of Boconnoc for his services.

As a result of all this intercession, the deputies were again summoned before Burghley, who told them that 'her Ma: ᵗⁱᵉ pleasure was that the leases should be reuoked and no more such graunted.' One at least of the deputies, probably Carew, was not so carried away by jubilation as to forget to ask the Lord Treasurer to let them have the Queen's decision in writing, and soon afterwards they received a note signed by Burghley 'Att the Court at Greenwitch this 21th of May 1594.'

The Queen, it read, had received the most humble supplication of Mr Richard Carew, Mr Jonathan Trelawny and others, and graciously commanded her Lord Treasurer to revoke all leases contrary to the old custom of tenure. But, he added, she had also ordered him to consider the nature of their suit, and he still maintained that there was no custom to prevent the Queen's making the best profit she could. However, 'Her Ma: ᵗⁱᵉ of her speciall goodness and princely fauour which she beareth to all her auncient tenauntes of the Duchie mindeth to use them with all reasonable fauour and continue them as her tenauntes without exacting any unreasonable fines.' And now, Burghley concluded, Her Majesty requires you all to go home.

Burghley had a way of tempering Elizabeth's generosity, no doubt in collusion with the Queen herself, though in this case he must have taken particular pleasure in deflating the success of Essex's intervention. In any event, to the deputies 'the worde "unreasonable" incerted herein seemed to be such indeede'; although the ancient form of tenure was to be retained, the Duchy officials could raise their rents at will. They hurried to 'their oracle', Sir Henry Killigrew, who, however, advised them 'not to stur ouermuch about it, lest the Lord Treasurer (not easely drawne from his once taken course) might take some conceite against them', and most of the deputies, their former elation somewhat qualified by this 'unreasonable' word, returned to Cornwall.

Carew, Trelawny and John Nance, however, remained to renew their suit at the beginning of June, when they asked Burghley to fulfil his promise to revoke the leases. But they met with another reverse, for before this could be done, they were told, the expenses of Edwards and the other lessees must be paid. The outraged deputies replies 'that the tenauntes would not very willingly disburse ought to him who had bene the author of their troubles,' and when they dared to mention again the question of the tenant custom, Burghley 'somewhat angerly answeared that they had no custome.' They fared no better with Fortesque, Chancellor of the Exchequer, who had 'also altered into rougher termes . . . and, with a short congey, dismissed them.' However, they had the satisfaction of seeing the lessees equally discomfited, for when Edwards presented his petition that he might retain his lease, he was 'greeted with a sharpe welcom', and the wretched Megges, exhibiting his petition as Burghley 'was coming downe the stayres . . . receiued the title of a shifting fellowe, which,' Carew added, 'there proved partly trewe, for that he shifted off the hearing of the same by the reason of his thicklistednes.'

When, soon afterwards, Edwards sent in a claim of £240 for his expenses, the deputies wrote to Burghley protesting against this exorbitant demand (about £7,000 today), for, they maintained, the leases had been got under false pretences, and 'the tenauntes are beggered in following the suite'. There followed a meeting in Burghley's Westminster garden, when the parties almost came to blows; 'Mr Megges was againe bitterly reproued,' as was also one of the deputies, and when they offered to follow Burghley, who withdrew to consider the sum that the lessees were entitled to, 'he chid them away.' 'This delay grewe alike tegious to both parties. Whereon the deputes offered Edwards 100 markes [£67] in consideracion of his charges, but that he would not smell unto.'

To add to their troubles, Mr Maynard, who had acted on their behalf, hurt his leg and had to take to his bed, and Burghley set off for Theobalds, his Hertfordshire home, to prepare to receive the Queen, who had gone on her summer progress. Carew waylaid him as he went to his coach, and though Burghley admitted that 'he liked not thexcesse of Edwards demaund,' and Carew assured him that both parties would accept his decision, he refused to act as arbitrator, saying that they must agree among themselves.

After an attempt to bluff Edwards, on 13 June the deputies wrote from the Strand to Burghley's secretary, Mr Hickes, who had warned them that his lordship 'could in noe wise brooke to be troubled with suitors' at Theobalds. Accordingly they began apologetically, 'As wee are loath to importune the Lord Treasurer, being now busied with affaires of thestate and thentertaynment of her Ma: ^{tie},' and went on to say that all they wanted was a decision as to how much they should pay Edwards, and an Exchequer decree revoking the noxious leases, without mention of their ancient customs, which might now be misinterpreted to their prejudice.

By return Hickes sent them two letters from Burghley. One ordered them to raise £240 for Edwards from the Duchy tenants; the other was an open letter—'that you may read it and seale it upp afterwards,' wrote Hickes—to the Lord Chief Baron of the Exchequer, Sir William Periam, asking him to prepare a decree 'that the tenauntes shall renewe their leases according to their auncyent customes and for a fine arbitrarye at her Ma: ^{tie} pleasure.' There was a postscript: 'Tomorrowe this poore howse wilbe called ye q' house.' In other words, the Queen would arrive at Theobalds on the 14th, and no business would be transacted so long as she was there.

Not unnaturally, the letter to the Lord Chief Baron 'drew the deputes into a peck of doubts', for it was clean contrary to what they had asked for: nothing about revocation, and much about their ancient customs, their rents now becoming liable to increase at pleasure. Some of the deputies argued that they should not deliver the letter, but Sir Henry Killigrew 'told them it was daungerous to shuffle councellours letters,' and that evening they took it to Periam, asking him, however, to ignore it, and saying that they would rely on the Queen's word that the leases would be revoked. Periam was sympathetic, and promised to try to prevent the granting of any more leases, though Edwards, he added, must be paid.

The deputies had done all they could. It was nearly seven weeks since they had begun their journey, and now they turned for home. It would be almost midsummer when Carew reached Antony, where he spent the next fortnight writing his report. Summarizing the position, he struck a balance: some of our customs have been threatened; we have no decree revoking the leases; we must pay money to our adversaries; our rents may be raised. On the other hand: the chances are that we shall still enjoy our ancient customs; a decree would not bind the Queen; the money we must pay appears to be for legitimate expenses; the alteration of our rents 'is builded only upon a perhapps.' On the whole, he concluded, 'wee leave our cause in better terms than wee receiued it.'

The attempt to raise the £240 for Edwards was pursued with little enthusiasm, and at the beginning of December Carew received a letter from Somerset House. It was from Burghley, demanding the speedy settlement of the debt, 'with some reasonable farther consideracion' for Edwards, who had been put to more expense by their default.

Trelawny had been away, and it was 17 February 1595 before Carew sent him a copy of his report and asked him to try to collect the money in his area: 'The shortnes of the tyme urgeth your assistance with the more hast.' Yet it was 3 May before they wrote to Burghley, telling him that some of the tenants refused to pay, 'Whence ensueth that Mr Edwards cannot be satisfied throughly.' By return came a letter from the Court at Greenwich: 'After my very harty commendacions . . . these are to pray and require you to call all such as refuse before you and to moue them againe to contribute. . . Which, if they shall againe refuse to doe, then to lett them knowe from me that . . . they shalbe barred to renewe their leases according to their custome. . . Your very lo: frend William Burleigh.' Another letter three weeks later told them that Edwards would be compensated out of the increased rents of the defaulters.

Here the correspondence ends. Edwards got his money, the leases were revoked, and the tenants retained their ancient customs. But in the *Survey* Carew wrote with unaccustomed venom: 'since which time this barking dog has been musled. May it please God to award him an utter choking, that he never have power to bite again.' Yet it was only a variation on the Queen's own words: 'I would they weare hanged who haue bene the doers hereof.'

Carew had another important journey to make in 1594: to take young Richard to Oxford, and see him safely established as an undergraduate.

3

Richard Carew the Younger

Thirty-four years later, Richard was to write a book for the edification of his children. Fortunately, however, it was not confined to edification, for though God may be said to be the chief character in the story, there is much about himself and his family; and what he has to say is not only interesting in itself, but also a revelation of the man who was the link between his famous father and the two sons who were to play their parts in history. He begins with his early childhood.

'In mine infancy (before I knew danger) it pleased Almighty God twice to preserve my life, when death came so near unto me and so inevitably (as I have been told) as I believe few have escaped the like. Once, when being in my coats according to the delight of that age, I went to look for babies in a water-pit, into which when the weight of my head was drawing the rest of my body after, God sent a servant of the house in the instant of my falling, to catch me by my coats and to save me.

'Another time, when I was playing in the entry, one having unadvisedly left a piece charged in the kitchen, another, thinking only to make sport with it, took up the piece, levelled it at me, pulls up the cock, puts down the hammer, and calling to me, "Now, master, have at you!" moves the trigger, meaning to give fire in jest, when off goes the piece in earnest, and the shot lights upon one of the pillars fast by me, God having by the sudden flash of the fire (ere he was aware) diverted the mouth a little from me.'

34

There were even greater perils than death by accident lurking about the servants' quarters at Antony House in his childhood. 'Being asked one morning whether my hands were clean or no, I answered I thought they were, because I had done nothing with them since I washed them. I was desired to show them, when, having showed the back side of my right hand, supposing it had been to have seen the honey-speck thereon I was born with, the other was presently asked for, and showing the back side thereof, the other side was demanded and suddenly put into a woman's hand who stood by there (no way suspected by me) to utter her cunning, whom God would not suffer to look on it, by making her eyes goggle in her head when she offered to do it, and making me presently (when I knew the intention) to withdraw it, and answer: "I will no fortunes, I thank you; for the good, it will come fast enough of itself; for the bad, either there is no truth or no remedy. I will leave it to God Almighty; it hath ever turned to mischief to those who have had to do withal." '

The chief playmates of Richard's childhood were his sister Gertrude and his brother, a second John, but he must often have seen two other small boys of about his own age, who lived at Halton, between Antony and Cotehele. Halton was 'the pleasant and commodious dwelling' of his father's great friend, Anthony Rous, whose son Francis was a year older than Richard, and whose stepson John Pym, for he married twice, was a year or two younger. Again, not far away, at St Germans, was a third boy destined to play a part in history, John Eliot, though he was too young to be one of Richard's early companions.

His father, as we should expect, brought him up sensibly, without coddling: 'Neither was I so daintly bred but that by my father's appointment, in heat, cold and wet, in frost and snow, I followed my play and my sports bareheaded.' And again, 'My father (from my childhood) took all the care he could to have me bred up in learning, well knowing the value thereof by the sweet fruits he still gathered of his own, which he always increased by his (almost incredible) continual labour;

35

for without a teacher he learned the Greek, Dutch [German], French, Spanish and Italian tongues, and to this end placed me with the best teachers he either knew or could hear of by any of his friends.'

Richard was proud of his father, and always spoke of him with affection and reverence: 'A father, God gave me, derived out of an ancient and noble family, of which some of our ancestors have descended from the royal race, and himself so excellent for his virtues, which made him justly esteemed no way unworthy of his best fortunes; a man in whom I ever found so much good and so little evil, as if it had been in mine own power to have chosen among all the men that ever I knew whom I listed for a father, I could not tell where to ask such another, and continually so loving unto me and mine as I could with no reason desire more. His wisdom doth well appear in his writings, his conversation so full of sweetness as was able to gain everybody's affection, and as sure a keeper by his constant loving honesty as an assured getter by his ever ready courtesy, it being always his greatest desire to do good, and his greatest joy when he could do it; who still sought to overcome his enemies rather by returning them courtesies than revenging their injuries; even more careful of the public good than of his own private, so as I fear succeeding times will make his loss to be no less lamented by his country in general than by his family in particular; so upright in matters of justice that they raised a common proverb upon him, that he was the worst friend and best enemy in all the country, because he would do no more than justice for the one, nor no less for the other.'

It was not from his father that he learned to make pert answers like that to the fortune-teller whose eyes goggled in her head when she seized his hand, or to consider himself one of the elect, sometimes, indeed, almost chosen by God to be His mouthpiece; for he concludes his anecdote: 'These words God made me suddenly to speak; neither once only have I found myself made to give such answers as I must ever acknowledge to have proceeded from a greater power than any I have in mine own will, though it pleased God to give them by my mouth.' The mischief seems to have been done by one of his early tutors, 'amongst which I must never forget one, though I can scarce remember his name, which if I mistake it not it was Robinson, who took care not only to teach his scholars humane knowledge, but the only true knowledge, which concerns God and our souls. Every Saturday, a little after dinner, he used to exhort us, what true joy every good Christian receives by the grace of God, which unspeakable comfort can be communicated to none but to the chosen children of God in Christ.'

As a result the precocious little boy constantly felt that he was being watched, even when he went to feed the fishes in his father's saltwater pond beside the Lynher: 'When in the pleasant summer evening I went alone through the orchard to feed them, looking about me and seeing the trees, they seemed to me as if they would prove so many witnesses of my thoughts which I had when I was at that time among them.' Sometimes he was asked, presumably by Robinson, what he had seen: 'whereunto I answered that I saw the greater fishes with their own overeagerness lose the meat which the lesser got by coming gently unto it, when the others had with their own sudden violence thrust it away from them. Wherein, methought, they resembled such persons as could not be contented with the ordinary means God hath appointed for us to attain our desires, but, forsaking them, seem to amend their fortune by a vain confidence they may do it by help of such as wickedly undertake to tell it.'

Thus the years passed for Richard at Antony. He was eight at the time of the Armada, when God, having 'let us see our own weakness, took the cause into his own hand,' and so terrified the Spaniards with fire-ships that 'they cut their cables and lost their anchors, and were so dispersed by the wind and sea as very few of that almighty fleet had ever the power to return home again.' His father, busy writing his *Survey of Cornwall*, had inspired in him 'a great delight in histories, for therein, methought, I might easily in a short space find the most precious treasures the wisest men could gather, and it was a great comfort unto me, that though there was an impossibility for me to be acquainted with their persons, yet I had a pleasing admittance by their writings to know their minds.'

When he was thirteen he was made 'master of his own purse', and in the following year, the year of the Duchy Suite, he went up to Oxford, where he matriculated from Merton College on 10 October 1594. Francis Rous was already there, and John Pym followed a few years later, both of them having rooms, like Richard's father, in Broadgates Hall. Richard's tutor was a young man, 'one Mr Christopher Dale, who took great care both to teach us the knowledge of the arts, and also to show us how their true and best profit was to be found in the right service of Almighty God.' He did, however, read some profane authors, and it was now that he discovered Plato and Socrates, 'who was in his time worthily esteemed the wisest man of all Greece, who so freely bestowed such excellent instructions, not only on his friends, but also on all persons he could get opportunity to do any good unto; such an excellent art as seemed nothing but pure simplicity until the conclusion discovered the cunning.' Then he adds the disarming confession: 'But perhaps mine own natural inclination to his kind of arguings, as well as my weak desire of imitation, must excuse the imperfection of my judgment.' It was true enough: Richard had a weakness for cunning Socratic arguings, and for freely bestowing his excellent instructions on all those who would listen to him.

His father, uncle George and grandfather had all been students of the Middle Temple, and to that Inn of Court, after little more than two years at Oxford, 'Richard Carewe, son and heir of Richard Carewe of Antony, Cornwall, esq.' was admitted on 17 February 1597. It was an exciting year in which to be in London: the year of the Islands Voyage, when the Earl of Essex and Raleigh sailed to the Azores in an attempt to intercept the Spanish treasure fleet on its return from America; of another invasion scare; of the production of the 'seditious and sclanderous' *Isle of Dogs* at the new Swan theatre, and of *Romeo and Juliet* at the Curtain. For a few pence Richard could have picked up a first edition of the play—though, like *Godfrey of Bulloigne*, a pirated one—and copies of the newly published tragedies about his namesakes, *Richard II* and *Richard III*. The young braves of the Inns of Court were among the principal supporters of the theatre, as Tom Nashe, main author of the *Isle of Dogs*, tells us: 'For whereas the after-noone beeing the idlest time of the day; wherein men that are their owne masters (as Gentlemen of the Court, the Innes of the Courte, and the number of Captaines and Souldiers about London) do wholly bestow themselves upon pleasure, and that pleasure they devide either into gameing, following of harlots, drinking, or seeing a Playe: is it not better that they should betake them to the least extreame, which is Playes?' But it is difficult to imagine Richard spending his afternoons in gaming, wenching and beerbathing. At all events, he makes no mention of such pastimes, though admittedly we should not expect him to do so in a book written for the edification of his children and Christian brethren, and his only comment about his life in the Middle Temple is: 'I well remember how I as soon grew weary of my too great liberty as before I had been greedy of it.'

His father joined him in London in the autumn, when he was one of the representatives of the little borough of Mitchell in the Parliament that met in October. He brought with him the manuscript of a poem, which was published a few months later as 'A Herrings Tayle: Containing a Poeticall fiction of divers matters worthie the reading.' He modestly withheld his name, even his initials, and the only external evidence of his authorship is a reference in John Guillim's *Display of Heraldry* (1610): 'albeit the Snaile goeth most slowly, yet in time, by her constancie in her course, she ascendeth the top of the highest Tower, as that worthy and learned gentleman Master Carew of Antony hath wittily moralized in his poeme intituled, *the hearings taile*.' But there is no mistaking the style: the vocabulary, jingles, racy colloquialisms, humour and high spirits are all unmistakably Carew's, as is the fantastic story compounded of Arthurian romance and the *Natural History* of his great favourite, Pliny; the scene at once Tintagel and Antony, where 'the bastard brackish wave' of Tamar and Lynher is neither salt nor fresh. The poem has nothing to do with herrings, but is the mock-heroic story of how the Cornish snail, Sir Lymazon, scales the steeple of a mausoleum raised by Merlin at Tintagel:

> And whereso art or fortune taught or brought his ways,
> A varnish on his footsteps smooth and bright he lays,
> Smooth as the path which under walking fingers yields,
> And twixt two hillocks leads unto th' Elysian fields.

At the top he finds Alectravemos, the weathercock, and after a fearful battle defeats him and mounts his head. His eyes are dazzled by the prospect that they see, the countryside, the cattle and the people:

> They see old folk knock with their staff at gate of grave,
> But though forward their pace, froward their face they have;
> They see young folk dancing a round to pipe of time,
> Whiles at their back steals in the just reward of crime,
> And with his dart strikes one: he falls, the others fear
> And stand a space amaz'd: some out the carcass bear,
> And they begin afresh, and so continue on,
> Till one by one thus fetcht, the dancers all be gone.

He dreams of conquest, but Aeolus, 'god of puffs' and father of Alectravemos, sends forth his winds, and

> the alter'd heavens were overlaid
> With mourning black, as in their limits should be play'd
> A tragedy, for which a stage they 'gan prepare.

(Carew was no stranger to the London theatres, and knew the convention of draping the 'heavens', the canopy over the stage, with black when a tragedy was to be performed.) 'So whilst in sea of bliss he sailéd all aflaunt', Lymazon is assailed:

> the winds wedge-wise in drive
> Their blasts, and stitch by stitch his clibby belly rive,

and down he falls, and with him fall 'his hopes, his plots, his pranks, his joy and jollity'.

A Herring's Tail, though not one of the greatest, is one of the gayest and most entertaining poems of the period, a *jeu d'esprit*, 'a poeticall fiction of divers matters worthie the reading'.

In the same year, probably owing to the influence of his old friend Camden, who was still urging him to finish his *Survey*, Carew was elected a member of the Society of Antiquaries, to which he delivered a paper on the history of Cornish agriculture. No doubt he stayed with his brother George, who had just been appointed ambassador to Poland, and, anxious to give his son, Richard, the advantage of foreign travel which he himself had missed, arranged for him to accompany his uncle.

'From the Middle Temple,' wrote young Richard, 'I went with my uncle (when he was sent Ambassador to the King of Poland) into Germany and Sweden, in which journey we escaped many great dangers, God (of his great mercy) having reserved us to other ends.' Even his father admitted that they 'underwent extraordinary perils'. When they arrived at Danzig they found that Sigismund III of Poland had just sailed for Sweden at the head of an army in an attempt to regain the crown usurped by his uncle, and hearing that the campaign was likely to be a short and successful one they followed him. Apparently they were involved in the battle on the river Stångå, for Richard tells how, 'When I was in Sweden, where a battle was fought by a river, more were drowned there by running into the water than were slain by the enemy.' He elaborates the story in one of his more purple passages: 'What a terrible thing it is when nation riseth against nation, and cometh armed against each other with fire, sword and deadly hatred, madly provoking one another for vain glory; entering into the battle with rich apparel, gilded arms, great scarfs and feathers, and with the loud sounding music of the rattling drums, shrill trumpets, and all sorts of warlike instruments; where the musket spits out his hissing bullet, and the thundering cannon roars and tears armed men; where the sword hews in pieces man's flesh, as butchers do beasts in their shambles; where men beg it as a favour to be rid of their lingering tormenting lives by a speedy death.' Sigismund was defeated, and, after following him back to Poland, Richard and his uncle returned to England in 1599.

'A little after my return I went over into France with Sir Henry Neville, who was sent there Ambassador Lieger.'

Neville was an elderly diplomat who had Cornish connections, his wife being the cousin of John Killigrew of Arwennack, Falmouth, who contrived to combine the office of Captain of Pendennis Castle with the more lucrative vocation of piracy. In 1599, therefore, Carew arranged that Richard should accompany the new ambassador to France, so that he might 'learn the French tongue', which eventually he did, though to begin with he was driven to make himself understood in Latin.

Richard was almost as much concerned with the health of his body as he was with the health of his soul, and in the little medical book that he was to write nearly forty years later he has much to say about his physical condition when in France, though nothing about the condition of the country, which, under Henry IV, had just emerged from forty years of civil and religious war.

'When I went into France, being much subject to flushing heats, I feared wine would inflame me, therefore drank water all the way from Dieppe towards Paris, which, whiles I exercised my body with travelling, my journeys made me costive, but when I came to rest at Paris brought me to a far more offensive looseness, and much pain with the colic. Continuing also awhile in a place where the drink was sour, knowing all sour things to be contrary to my nature, to avoid the inconvenience thereof I used milk instead of drink at my meals, but the coldness bound me so hard that when I went to stool I buttoned like a rabbit, and yet could very seldom ease myself without the force and help of my fingers, though the natural constitution of my body hath always been too soluble, and the greatest imperfection of my stomach hath been want of sufficient retention.'

Unhappily he also suffered from spots. 'In my youth I was subject to outward inflammations, which I supposed came from too much heat of my stomach, but by a due observation of the true cause of this infirmity I perceived it proceeded from the coldness of my stomach, which being oppressed therewith, made my liver to break out with a violent and unnatural heat, as we see and know that those who handle snow find not so great a coldness in the beginning as a violent heat and swelling after, when nature returns with force to expel her enemy, which had entered by cold into the flesh and blood. The first light of this I received from Sir Henry Neville, at Orleans in France, who observing me at supper with him, in my drink to use very much water and little wine, told me very kindly (for he was a truly noble and courteous gentleman, and gained much honour by his brave carriage during the time of his whole ambassage) that he doubted much I committed the same error which himself had done, seeing my neck full of red pimples (as my whole body was likewise then), and said that he thought the cause of my inflammation proceeded rather from the coldness of the water than the heat of the wine I drank.'

The poor boy—he was only nineteen—seems to have had an unhappy time in France. 'A while after I came to Orleans I had an ague, and was persuaded for the recovery of my health to use the help of a physician who, to cure me thereof, as he did, gave me a purge which he told me would cause half a dozen stools, but when I had taken it I found the operation thereof so much stronger upon my body than I thought it would have been, as it gave me thirty, with such extreme pain as it made me then to consider with myself whether there could be any grievouser torturing death devised than the scouring and tearing of the guts by the windiness and fretting of purging.'

He never forgot this purge at Orleans, and the moral was to avoid all doctors and 'the common practice of physic, in giving preparatives, vomits, purges, clysters and blood-letting, because they are all weakeners of nature,' for every man best knows his own body and is his own best physician. Above all, keep warm, both within and without, for 'cold is a great cause of costiveness, which is very unwholesome, and more unwholesome if it be so great as to make a looseness. Comfortable liquor, good ale, beer or wine, heat as hot as I could well drink it without scalding, hath, as far as I can find, been the natural means of the preservation of my health.' Certainly his reasoning was logical enough: 'that nothing received into the stomach can turn into nourishment but by heat, that the thing itself being warmed by the fire easeth the stomach of much labour and, enables it by this help to perform what nature requires, which otherwise it could not do.'

Sir Henry Neville was a man after Richard's own heart, but he was not altogether happy in his embassy; although he negotiated a valuable treaty, he was poorly received by the French, who called him a Puritan, and on the pretext of being troubled with deafness he asked to be recalled. Shortly after his return he was implicated in Essex's rebellion of February 1601, fined and dismissed from his offices, and though pardoned by James I he forfeited preferment by his democratic opinions both in politics and religion.

So, towards the end of 1600 Richard returned to England with a knowledge of French and a truer understanding of his stomach and liver. His return to Antony was celebrated in Latin verse by his friend Charles Fitzgeoffrey, rector of St Dominic, the parish church of Halton, to which living he had recently been presented by Anthony Rous. He had been a contemporary of Richard and of Francis Rous at Oxford, and gained a modest celebrity by a poem on the death of Sir Francis Drake, and by the inclusion of a number of his pieces in the miscellany, *England's Parnassus*. His Latin epigrams, containing that on Richard and another on his father, were published in 1601, the year in which Richard's brother John, only a boy, lost his hand at the siege of Ostend, returning with it and throwing it on the table with, 'This is the hand that cut the pudding at dinner.'

By this time his father had almost completed the final version of his *Survey of Cornwall*. He was only forty-five, but had never been strong, and Richard tells us: 'My father (himself having been a ward) was desirous to see me married before I was twenty-one, fearing by reason of his often sickness'—he suffered from a rupture and a chronic cough—'he should have died before I was of full age, albeit I wanted not a quarter of a year, when by the motion of our friends and consent of our parents I married Mistress Bridget Chudleigh of Ashton in the county of Devon.' That was in January 1601. Bridget brought

44

him a dowry of £1,500 (some £40,000 of our money), and a settlement was drawn up and signed by father and son, one of the trustees being Richard's young uncle, John Arundell of Trerice. Carew arranged to give Richard an annuity of £60 (some £1,600 a year) and with a sober satisfaction completed the account of his family in the manuscript of his *Survey*: '. . . Richard, lately wedded to Bridget, daughter of John Chudleigh of Ashton in Devon.' Bridget's father had died soon after her birth, leaving another daughter Dorothy, who became the third wife of Sir Reynold Mohun of Boconnoc, and a son George, who married the daughter of Sir William Strode of Newnham, Devon, uncle of Francis Rous and John Pym. The Carew contacts and alliances were becoming increasingly liberal and puritanical.

4

Bridget Chudleigh

Bridget was as affectionate as she was beautiful, as dutiful a wife—almost—as Richard could have wished, though apparently even more serious-minded than himself. 'A woman of a most mild and modest behaviour, that for her person and conditions might have given content to a prince; so loving and respective to me continually as I could even almost wish; so kind to all my kindred and friends, as she was no less beloved of them than of her own; so careful to please my parents and every one of our family by her fair and respective behaviour; so desirous to do any good office to any of our neighbours; so glad to take any pains for any of them if it lay any way in her power to do them good; so careful to avoid the least offence; so diligent to attend the public service of God, and so duly observing her set times for her private devotion; so zealous in her prayers, as my father observed he had scarce heard the like' (one scents a note of disapproval here) 'and all her conversation every way suitable; so diligent to teach our children the fear of God, as she was loth to spare me one hour in a day to be merry with her, lest she should not have time enough to instruct them, and even angry with them if she found their children less able or willing to learn than she was to teach.'

Richard was the most prudent of young men, and gave much thought to the best way of investing his capital, not an easy matter to decide when he had a puritanical dislike of 'laying out money to use', that is, of lending money at interest, though he was not without hope that his virtue would have its reward.

'As soon as I was married I began to think of preparing for such children as I hoped God would send me. I have been master of my own purse ever since I was thirteen years old, and before I had a growing charge I sought not to gather, but at the year's end made an even reckoning, neither owing nor leaving. But when after my marriage I had the full means I was to expect for my maintenance during my father's life, I told my wife my parents were young, and therefore like to live long, and that it was our duty to pray they might; how I hoped we should have children, which as they grew would require more from us for their maintenance, therefore I held it fit to spend but half of what we had, for if we should save nothing in the beginning while we were young, what should we do when we were old and needed more? To which she very willingly agreed'—'and then I bethought myself how I might employ the little I could spare, to make it be my care to increase with my charge, and though I saw laying out money to use then to be a very common and easy trade, yet I would not meddle with it for fear of offending God thereby, for that I believed and said that He was not so poor but once in seven years He could and would do me as good turn as ten in the hundred came to, if for conscience' sake I forbore it.' God, in a word, was good for ten per cent to the virtuous. 'Neither do I repent it, for I find by just accounts that if the money my father and myself have duly paid for use had been as duly laid to use, it would have amounted to above £150,000'—an almost incredible sum. 'For what', he concludes, 'should it avail a man to get never so much, and leave the plague of God with it to his posterity?'

His father's chief delight was his 'fishful pond', and Richard found a similar enchantment in his orchards, which had the additional advantage of solving his investment problem and yielding a profitable return, particularly when he discovered the way to perpetuate a variety of tree without further grafting, and here follows one of the most charming passages in his book. 'I therefore fell to planting of fruit trees, making that my delight, and, I thank God, as merrily I passed my time therein as if I had done it in hawking or hunting; and my apple trees I called my hounds, and my pear trees my hawks, and I hope I can show twenty thousand of them which have all passed through my hands, besides thousands which I gave away.'

The Bible, of course, proved the best handbook to fruit growing, Genesis being particularly helpful on the culture of the apple. 'My best instructions I had in this kind, as in all things else, is to be had out of the Scripture, wherein I found the only food God appointed man in his innocency was the fruit of the tree, that when he placed him in Paradise he appointed him to dress the garden; by the parable of the vine and fig tree in the Gospel, pruning and dressing it proved to be necessary if we will look for fruit; in Job, how a tree, quailed and dried by the roots, by the scent of water in seasonable time, may be recovered; all of which I have still found to be true by mine own experience.'

The innocent enjoyment that he found in fruit-tree growing broadened into a general interest in natural history. Francis Rous's grandfather, Thomas Southcote of Bovey Tracey, who died in 1600, had encouraged him to persevere in his pursuit of knowledge, and he was by nature curious, an acute observer and, like his father, astonished by the wonder of the world. A hundred years later Anthony Wood was to write that Carew was 'the most excellent manager of bees in Cornwall', but, as in so many other ways, Wood confused the two Richards, and there can be little doubt that it was the son, not the father, who had that reputation. It is doubtful if anybody else at this time knew as much about the habits of bees as Richard, a thing that particularly interested him being how they 'die of a looseness' if they eat a mixture of old and new honey.

'I took delight also in keeping bees, pheasants, partridges, small birds, silkworms and fishes, out of whose secret natures I still desired to discover something more than ordinary, which methought a little care made easy to be done, though I always endeavoured to get the best authors I could hear of, and talk with the most experienced men I could meet with in any of these kinds, and ever found a rule of the old Mr Southcote's to be true, that every man of reasonable capacity finds so much more by every latter seven years' experience, that he was a fool in the former, because he might well have made better use of them. And when I had learned as much as I thought I might conveniently do in one kind, I left that and proceeded to another, not out of an inconstancy, as some would charge me with, but that I might be doing more good, and always marvelled that most of our famous authors have delivered many things for truth which were none, and neglected strange and pleasing ones which I wondered how they missed, being so apparent.

'In bees I observed that they do but gather their honey and pour it into their little holes, and then seal it up, and how they both gather and make their wax by moulding it with their pincer-like mouths, and how when any one begins to gather honey or wax out of any flower he very seldom changes from the kind with which he begins, though there be divers kinds in the field, of which each several bee makes his particular use. They never swarm till their hives be fully furnished with combs, and thereby perceive their want of room to continue together, and those which issue out go not away without carrying competent provision with them to maintain them till they can get new; which I have seen so consumed by continual foul weather that they have starved thereby within seven nights they were swarmed. In their fighting they never offer to sting one another, but strive to pinch in the narrow place which joins the fore and hinder part together, knowing perfectly that a bee so bitten can never fly any more, and therefore must die quickly. The swallows are their cruel enemies, and watch to take them as they fly, and feed upon them; and this little fly, which only lives upon the beautiful sweetness of flowers would yield pleasing matter for a pretty tract.'

Quickened by the excitement of describing his observations and discoveries, he writes at his best, and for the time quite forgets that he is writing for the edification of his young family.

'A couple of pheasants I made so tame as, though I gave them the liberty of the field, yet when I whistled for them, they would presently come to me to take meat out of my hand.

Which bird hath strange qualities: he never crows as long as he hath a hen in sight, but when he would have her he then imperiously with his voice, shaking his wings and turning on his toe, requires her to come unto him morning and evening, and is seldom disobeyed. When they meet they run in a path as fast and as far as they can, each before other by turn, for almost a quarter of an hour, when suddenly the cock flies eagerly at the hen, and she makes all the shift she can to escape him, and when she is taken squeaks for fear, and he violently oppresses her. At noon they use to bask in the dust, and the cock comes to the hen, setting himself forth in his greatest bravery, stretching out his red gills, bowing his neck, bunching his back like a camel, spreading his train on one side, and thus approaching her shaking it, offers to take her by the neck as if he would tread her, when she skips two or three foot off and falls to basking again, which denial the cock seems to take with the indignity of a grumbling voice, yet renews the play again, but in that sort never comes to it in earnest. Their chickens, I have seen, within an hour they have come into the field, presently go to the froth which in the summer hangs on the bushes, and thence to pick out the grasshoppers which live therein, and eat them, which was strange to see how the instinct of nature could teach them to find that food they could not see.

'The partridge in his kind differs far from the pheasant, for when he purposes to tread, he steals so softly after the hen as if he meant not to be perceived, and the hen lies down so close before him as if she would not be seen, when the cock in the height of his pride, foot after foot, all by leisure gets on her, and when he hath done, stretches himself to his utmost length and crows. Yet I could never have any breed, because they had been bred wild.'

The life-cycle of silkworms affords visible and almost metaphysical evidence of the resurrection and immortality of the soul. 'In silkworms I found so many wonderful changes wrought by such insensible degrees to such different forms as at last have no kind of resemblance one to another (as thereby any man may plainly perceive how easy it is for Almighty God by the same incomprehensible power to transform these our souls from the earthly bodies He hath given us to the heavenly ones which He will in His due time give unto us). First they are eggs, and so continue for three quarters of a year without food or life, so as during all this season (as a dear friend of mine observed) there is not one of these worms to be found alive in the whole earth, yet when their time comes to take life by the natural heat of the year, or the artificial heat man gives unto them, their multitudes are innumerable, and they provide the best matter for the clothes of kings, princes and all the noble persons of the world. From an egg he turns to a caterpillar, and being a caterpillar changes three or four times, and every time leaves his skin behind him, and seeks a convenient place where to hang his silken grave, in which he buries himself for eight or ten days, and in this space is made a perfect butterfly, and hath yet remaining in him only one drop of moisture left to open a passage for him out of his grave, from which they arrive with great lustiness and nimbleness, and ply their new-curled wings, and apply themselves to breeding with as much eagerness as any creature can do; which being done, the male falls off dead, and the female survives only until she have shed her seed. And of this kind there was never widow in the world.'

There can have been very few such devoted naturalists at the beginning of the seventeenth century, and among the gentry, or as we should say, the county, there must have been some raising of eyebrows and facetious gossip about this serious-minded, high-principled young man, who preferred bird-watching, carp-breeding, bee-keeping and fruit-growing to hawking and hunting, who would rather observe the ways of animals than pursue and kill them.

While Richard was thus busy with his natural history, his father was finishing his *Survey*, begun twenty years before, and now laboriously concluded after a visit to Godolphin and the far west of the shire. 'Diogenes, after he had tired his scholers with a long Lecture, finding at last the voyde paper, Bee glad, my friends (quoth hee) wee are come to harbour. With the like comfort, in an vnlike resemblance, I will refresh you, who haue vouchsafed to travaile in the rugged and wearysome path of mine ill-pleasing stile, that now your iourney endeth with the land; to whose Promontory (by *Pomp. Mela,* called *Bolerium* . . . by the *Cornish Pedn an Laaz*: and by the English, The lands end) because we are arriued, I will heere sit mee downe and rest. *Deo gloria: mihi gratia.* 1602. April. 23.'

It was St George's Day, Shakespeare's thirty-eighth birthday. But Carew was nine years older than Shakespeare and, as we know from Richard, in poor health, and it must have been with genuine relief that he laid down his pen.

Richard had now been married for more than a year, and it was at about this time that Bridget gave birth to their first child, Elizabeth, named after her grandmother, Elizabeth Edgcumbe, and the Queen, now in her sixty-ninth year and beginning to fail. We can imagine the fussy young man directing preparations for the arrival of his daughter, making up the fire and seeing that everything was warm, and his satisfaction when he made Bridget comfortable after the birth: 'My wife, after she was delivered of mine eldest daughter, being put to sweat, complained unto me she could get no heat in her feet. I told her I would presently make her a medicine, thereupon warmed a broad thick stone that was apt to receive heat and retain it long, and, lapping it in a blanket, put it upright at the lower end of the bed, by which means she quickly and easily came to sweat as kindly as possibly could be.' It is the first mention of the famous warming-stone.

Another daughter, Martha, was born in the following year, probably at the beginning of James I's reign, for on 24 March 1603 Queen Elizabeth died and was succeeded by her grandnephew James VI of Scotland, who thus united the crowns of the two countries. Six weeks earlier, on 8 February, 'A booke called the Survey of Cornwall' had been entered in the Register of the Stationers' Company, and would be on sale a few days later at the Sign of the Hand and Star, near Temple Bar. (The date on the title page is 1602, but as in those days the year began on 25 March it was really 1603 according to our reckoning.) The publisher was John Jaggard, brother of William

Jaggard who, with his son Isaac, was to publish the First Folio of Shakespeare twenty years later.

It must be remembered that the great majority of Elizabethans knew less about England than most of us today know about, say, Manchuria or Tierra del Fuego, and that for a peasant living in the Midlands the Cornish coast was as inconceivable as the Nile valley or Cotopaxi. It is true that, for those who could afford to buy them, there were Christopher-Saxton's splendid maps of England and Wales, and, for those who could read, William Harrison's discursive *Description of Britain* and Camden's Latin *Britannia*, but the only detailed description of an English county before the publication of Carew's *Survey of Cornwall* was William Lambarde's *Perambulation of the County of Kent*. The *Survey*, therefore, is historically important, for in it Carew describes the agriculture, mining, fishing and local government of his time, and in greater detail the places and people 'of the former or later ages' in each of the nine hundreds of the shire. But more than this: it is also a minor Elizabethan classic, written in prose that many of his contemporaries must have envied, from the racy: 'Of all manner vermin, Cornish houses are most pestered with rats, a brood very hurtful for devouring of meat, clothes and writings by day; and alike cumbersome, through their crying and rattling, while they dance their gallop galliards in the roof at night,' to the studied eloquence of his tribute to a fifteenth-century John Arundell, who was killed in a skirmish on the sands, as had been foretold: 'So Cambyses lighted on Ecbatana in Egypt, and Alexander Epirot on Acheros in Italy, to bring them to their end. So Philip of Macedon, and Atis the son of Croesus, found a chariot in a sword's hilt, and an iron pointed weapon at the hunting of a boar, to delude their preventive weariness. So Hamilcar supped in Syracusa, and the Prince of Wales ware a crown thorough Cheapside, in another sort and sense than they imagined or desired. And so Pope Gerebert and our King Henry the Fourth travelled no farther for meeting their fatal Jerusalem, than the one to a chapel in Rome, the other to a chamber in Westminster.'

Carew mentions most of the gentry, many of them his friends and relations, for 'all Cornish gentlemen are cousins': his brother George, 'at this present a Master of the Chancery', his uncle Peter Edgcumbe, 'the now possessioner' of Mount Edgcumbe; his brother-in-law John Arundell, who 'inheriteth as well his father's love as his living', and future brother-in-law, the younger William Carnsew, 'to whose sounder judgment I owe the thankful acknowledgment of many corrected slippings in these my notes'; Anthony Rous, whose guests receive 'a kind and uninterrupted entertainment'; Sir Francis Godolphin, whose virtues 'have won him a very great and reverent reputation in his country'; Richard's brother-in-law, Sir Reynold Mohun of Boconnoc, 'one that by his courteous, just and liberal course of life maintaineth the reputation and increaseth the love always borne his ancestors', and a hundred more. The book was dedicated to his kinsman, Sir Walter Raleigh, Lieutenant General of Cornwall. Poor Raleigh: four months after its publication he was a prisoner in the Tower.

The portrait that emerges most clearly, however, is that of Carew himself. Not that it is a deliberate self-portrait, for he was the most self-effacing and elusive of writers, sometimes assuming the character of a third person to conceal his own generous actions, or the better to ridicule folly, as when, in the guise of 'a near friend' he makes fun of those killjoys who condemn saints' feasts as superstitious, church-ales as suggestive of dissipation, and the suffix 'mas' as smacking of popery. Let these precisians, he says, talk of church-beers or church-wines if they prefer it, of Christ-tide and Michael-tide, but if they are to be consistent they must also speak of Thomtide. A staunch Protestant, he was no bigot, and regretted the suppression of the free-schools and chantries because 'of a petty smack only of popery'. Nor did he fancy himself, like Richard, as another Socrates, by his cunning arguments convincing both friends and strangers of the error of their opinions. Wit and laughter were his weapons, and inhumanity was almost the only thing that made him angry. And, again unlike Richard, he would laugh at himself when he realized that he was on the verge of pomposity, as, more sceptical than credulous, lightly dismissing fortune-tellers as 'I wot not what calkers', he recorded the wonders and old-wives' tales of Cornwall.

He had his prejudices: his own class, the gentry, were rarely in the wrong, but most lawyers were to be distrusted, and Irish immigrants—Padstow was full of them—were little better than vermin. But of the Cornish people as a whole he always speaks with real affection, delighting in any eccentricity, and it was people, individual men and women, who interested him even more than the antiquities of Cornwall, even more perhaps, if that were possible, than Antony, his fishful pond and his beloved books. Slightly, and self-consciously, old-fashioned, he was essentially an Elizabethan, and regretted, one suspects, the transition to the laxer Jacobean age that the *Survey* ushered in, as he regretted the passing of the longbow in one of his most eloquent passages, where Archery herself defends the practice: 'Alas, what my desert can justify your abandoning my fellowship, and hanging me thus up to be smoke-starved over your chimneys? ... Am I unhandsome in your sight? Every piece of me is comely, and the whole keepeth an harmonical proportion... If I be praiseworthy, esteem me; if necessary, admit me; if profitable, employ me; so shall you revoke my death to life, and show yourselves no degenerate issue of such honourable progenitors.' Then, with a characteristic lapse into jest, Carew concludes: 'And thus much for Archery, whose tale, if it be disordered, you must bear withal, for she is a woman, and her mind is passionate.'

The accession of James I brought disaster to Raleigh, but preferment to Carew's brother George. Knighted by the king, he was appointed to the commission that arranged the new relationship between England and Scotland, and in 1605 became ambassador to the court of France. On his retirement from this office he wrote the important *Relation of the State of France*, and was rewarded with the lucrative post of Master of the Court of Wards.

The new reign made little difference to Richard, who now had a fascinating extension of natural history for his observations in the behaviour of his two young daughters, and it was from them that he learned the best remedy that he could ever find for the toothache, from which he suffered much at this time. Noting 'how much they vented by their noses of the abundance of rheum that offends the head,' in other words, how much their noses ran, he concluded that 'by the nose the best means might be used to draw away that rheum from the gums, which, having forced a passage there through that flesh, should naturally have vented itself by the nose, for that which is commonly taken for the aching of the teeth is in truth the pain of the flesh about them.' He therefore tried to draw his toothache through his nose with sneezing-powder, but this proving too violent a remedy, he experimented with tobacco, thin rolls of which he put up his nostrils. This soon drew the rheum that way, though it made him so dizzy that he staggered like a drunken man, his ears thundered, and when his stomach was oppressed with raw humours, it made him vomit. He would then lie down with a blanket over his head and a warming-stone at his feet, to make himself sweat, and in this way not only cured his toothache, but checked the decay of his teeth, and generally improved his health. The young heir to Antony was already well on his way to becoming an eccentric.

Soon after this, sometime in 1604, he found that his mother was expecting a tenth child, and he 'had somewhat to do to show a friend of mine how free I was from that general fault of elder brothers,' who resent any addition to their parents' family because it will reduce their inheritance. 'Among other talk, my friend told me of news which was reported abroad, that there was speech going how my mother was with child. That was near three years or more after my marriage, when God had given me two children, and my youngest sister was about five years of age, and in all that space my mother had had none between, and my parents themselves had given over expectation of any more'—yet Juliana was barely forty. 'Whereupon I was asked if it were true, and I said I thought it was. So when the party replied, "I am sorry for that, for it is likely to be a thousand pounds out of your way," I answered it should never be a thousand pins out of my way. I was then asked how this could be possible, saying if it were a maid, she would have a thousand pounds portion, and if it were a boy, a proportionable maintenance which must be raised out of the estate, which, after my parents' decease, was to come to me. When I still maintained I would have never a jot the less for all this, I was pressed to give my reason how it might be. Then I answered, "What God hath appointed for me shall surely come unto me; what God hath appointed for others I must as willingly let them have. Besides, be it brother or sister, I hope to have so much comfort thereby as I would be loth to lose such an one to get more by it; besides, I have two daughters of mine own, and I should take it ill at their hands if they should repine at a son which God should send me, because he would take away mine inheritance from them. And would not my parents have as just reason to condemn me if I should be unwilling to have them to have any more, as I could have for the same fault in my children? Nay, a great deal more, because mine are so little as by their age they cannot discern between good and ill, and I am a man." '

It is to be hoped that the virtuous young man really meant what he said, for God sent him a brother, Wymond. In the *Survey* his father had written:

> Children thrice three God hath vs lent,
> Two sonnes, and then a mayd,
> By order borne, of which, one third
> We in the graue haue layd.

Now he added another four lines in his own copy of the book:

> Our 10th childe, an unlooked sonne,
> After long respite came,
> And mee, who 9 times graundsire was,
> New gave a fathers name.

Not long afterwards Richard was able to prove how right he was about this matter of primogeniture. 'Once when a lady was talking to me, knowing me by my birth to be heir to my father, she began to complain on the law of the land, which gives all the inheritance to the eldest son, as it gives the whole kingdom to the heir of the king, for she said it was against all reason one child should have all, and the rest nothing. I answered, "That is true; therefore it appertaineth to the care and discretion of the father to make provision for his youngest children during his own life, whiles all is in his own hand." But being not contented with this answer, she replied, "Why should not all my husband's children have parts alike in his estate, as they are all alike his?" I answered again, "Madam, I think if there were such a law to be made you would be one of the first to speak against it." She told me she did not believe it. Then said I, "Your husband is an ancient gentleman, and the estate he now possesseth was not all of his own getting, but some he had from his father—" "Yes," says she—"and some from his grandfather, and some from his greatgrandfather's father, and divers other their forefathers." To which she answered it was all true. Then said I, "Madam, this equal division you would now have to be made should justly have begun among his children who got the first estate, and so still follow according to the same rule from father to son, until your husband come to receive no more than would be due unto him by this proportion, which, when you have restored the rest according to your own law, you may divide easily into as many parts as you please." After which time I never heard more of this kind of division.' Perhaps he had forgotten how his ancestor had inherited Antony.

Many years later, he added for the benefit of his children: 'How doth partiality, by the foolish and unjust affection we bear unto ourselves, deceive the judgment of the wisest and best of us all! And I have often thought how they be no less blind fools than most extremely wicked, who wish their parents' deaths that they may enjoy their estates; for by the same reason, one could no sooner receive according to his own damnable desire, but he must presently deliver it up by his death to his next successor.'

Whatever Richard really thought about the arrival of another brother, he desperately wanted a son of his own, and early in 1605 he came. They called him Nicholas, after the Carew whose marriage had brought Antony into the family, but he did not live long. He died in the early spring, in the season of primroses and daffodils, while Bridget was staying with her sister Dorothy Mohun. 'When our eldest son died, being near three months old, my wife was at Boconnoc with her sister, but I was here at home, the tenderness of whose heart because I well knew (though myself was very heartily sensible of the loss, and that it made me remember mine own sins, which it pleased God to punish by the death of that infant) I presently took horse and rode to her to comfort her, meaning to have concealed it awhile from her, and to have acquainted her by degrees in the best sort I might. But as soon as I came, I found her full of sorrow, and the first word she asked of me was, "Is my son dead?" To which question, being unwilling to give a direct answer, she pressed me so hard as I held it the best way to tell her presently the plain truth.' So far his conduct had been exemplary, but when poor Bridget broke down, what would she make of the young egotist's final consolatory words? 'When I found her apt to grieve too much, I told her I humbly thanked God that he had given *me* His grace to take this trial patiently, by which I was assured He would give me another son; if she too would be patient, it would be by her, if not, by somebody else.'

The next child, however, was another girl, Mary, born in 1607, and it was during this period of despondency after Nicholas's death that Richard was inspired by missionary zeal to consider going to America to convert the heathen natives. In 1605 three Indians had been brought to Plymouth, where they lived with the family of Sir Ferdinando Gorges, Governor of the Island and forts of the town. He was thus a near neighbour of the Carews at Antony, and Richard has a pathetic little story to tell of one of the Indians. 'When one of the natives was brought hither to Plymouth, as soon as he was landed he began (according to the directions given him by the lord of his country) to count the number of the persons he met with, and likewise the houses, with which being quickly wearied, he fell a-weeping; and being asked the cause, he said he had seen so many strange things that when he came to his country again they would not suffer him to sleep for their inquisitiveness to know what he had seen, and give him no rest by continual pressing him to answer their endless questions.'

In the following year Gorges became a member of the Plymouth Company, which had been granted the region of Maine, and it was largely owing to him that a party of settlers was sent out to establish itself at the mouth of the Kennebec river in 1607. It seems probable, therefore, that he was the friend who told Richard and his father of the proposed venture.

'When the country of these savages was discovered by some of our nation to be more inhabited by wild beasts than men, and that they found it to be a clime by nature apt to yield man more commodities than our own, if the like industry were there employed, and that many complained of our multitude, as if our land would within a while not suffice to maintain us, they thought it an honourable and profitable action to make a plantation there among them. In which, when a friend of mine was very earnest, I told him if this action was undertaken principally for the honour and glory of God, to teach these poor souls the right knowledge of the true God, He would then make it beneficial to the undertakers, but if that were but pretended, and gain intended, He would make them surely lose by it. To which, when he answered that it was purposed for the best end, I had a good will to have gone thither, but concealed it till I might know how my wife stood affected to my purpose. Whom, when I told what a noble action to advance the service of God was taken in hand, and that if I found reason to employ my person therein, whether she would leave our country, and our children to our friends, and go thither with me, she answered presently, "With all my heart." Then I bade her keep it secret (as she did) what I proposed unto her until I might look better into the true intention of the business, for I thought it not fit rashly, but upon good reason, to leave the place wherein I might do a little good, without fair hope to do more another where.

'Within a while there were instructions sent down from those of the east to their partners of the west'—that is, from London to Plymouth—'to set down the government they would have to be observed by this new colony, and they were by my fore-mentioned friend showed unto my father to have his advice therein, at which being present I observed the name of God had no place on the paper. Whereupon I had an utter discourage-ment to meddle with the matter, and told my friend I wished he would clear his hands as well as he might of this business, for that he would be assuredly a loser by it; and when I gave him my reason for it, he perused his papers again and sought for that name which he could not find there.'

Richard was right, the settlement was a failure. Supplies ran short, a severe winter was followed by the death of their leader, the colony was abandoned, and Richard was able to add the satisfactory note: 'I fear he hath lost a hundred, if not a thousand, pounds by it since.'

Richard's father was more interested in literature in England than in the conversion of the heathen in America, and at this time was writing a long letter to Camden, who published it in his *Remains of a Greater Work Concerning Britain* as *The Excellency of the English Tongue*. After describing the expressiveness and ease of English, Carew considers its delights: first its copiousness, its fabulous wealth of words, and then its sheer beauty of sound, lovingly concluding with the famous passage, which contains one of the first literary references to Shakespeare:

> I come now to the last and sweetest point of the sweetness of our tongue, which shall appear the more plainly if, like the London drapers, we match it with our neighbours. The Italian is pleasant, but without sinews, as a still-fleeting water. The French delicate, but even nice as a woman, scarce daring to open her lips for fear of marring her countenance. The Spanish majestical, but fulsome, running too much on the O, and terrible like the devil in a play. The Dutch [German] manlike, but withal very harsh, as one ready at every word to pick a quarrel. Now we, in borrowing from them, give the strength of consonants to the Italian, the full sound of words to the French, the variety of terminations to the Spanish, and the mollifying of more vowels to the Dutch, and so (like bees) gather the honey of their good properties, and leave the dregs to themselves. And thus when substantialness combineth with delightfulness, fulness with fine-

61

ness, seemliness with portliness, and courantness with staidness, how can the language which consisteth of all these sound other than most full of sweetness?

Again, the long words that we borrow, being intermingled with the short of our own store, make up a perfect harmony, by culling from out which mixture (with judgment) you may frame your speech according to the matter you must work on: majestical, pleasant, delicate or manly, more or less in what sort you please... Will you read Virgil? take the Earl of Surrey. Catullus? Shakespeare, and Marlowe's fragment. Ovid? Daniel. Lucan? Spenser. Martial? Sir John Davis and others. Will you have all in all for prose and verse? take the miracle of our age, Sir Philip Sidney.

Carew also told Camden that he was preparing a second edition of the *Survey*, 'not so much for the enlarging it, as the correcting mine and the printer's oversights, and amongst these the arms not the least.' Thus, in the copy to which he added the four lines on the birth of Wymond, he corrected 'manlike hunting vermin' to 'man-haunting vermin', and in his description of the arms of Vyvyan crossed out the meaningless 'unsase' and wrote 'undade' (*undée*, wavy). But, fastidious writer that he was, he also made a number of alterations for the sake of euphony, here transposing a phrase, there changing a word, 'wittes' to 'braines', for example, in order to relate it to 'sayles': 'But it was a windy knowledge that thus filled his sayles of glory, which grew at last so to tempest his braines, as he held Aristotle superior to Moses and Christ.' Then, as young William Carnsew had read his original manuscript, he would naturally send him the corrected copy of his book for any further alterations, and another hand, not as legible as Carew's, and presumably Carnsew's, has added a number of suggestions, mainly about north-east Cornwall, in the region of his home at Bokelly.

In his letter to Camden, Carew added: 'if I wist where to find Mr Norden I would also fain have his map of our shire, for perfecting of which he took a journey into these parts.' But it was to be more than a hundred years before a second edition of the *Survey* was published, and even longer before John Norden's *Description of Cornwall* appeared in 1728, 'with a Map of the

County and each Hundred; in which are contained the Names
and Seats of the several Gentlemen then Inhabitants: As also,
thirteen Views of the most remarkable Curiosities in that
County.' The maps are a delight, the views enchanting, and
among the names and seats of the gentlemen living in Cornwall
when Norden wrote in the early years of James I's reign is:

> *Antony* . . . the howse of a worthye gentleman called Mr. *Richard
> Carew*, whose learninge and deligence hath browghte fourth
> verie memorable thinges of his Natiue Countrie in Historye, and
> published it. The howse is profitablye and pleasantly seated:
> Below his howse, vpon the Creeke of the Sea, he hathe verie
> arteficially contryued a ponde of Salte water, and that stored
> with muche and greate varietye of good Sea-fishe.

But Antony was two hundred miles from London, and Carew
wrote to Sir Robert Cotton expressing his grief that his 'so remote dwelling' prevented his attending the meetings of the
'sweet and respected Antiquarian Society'. The older generation was failing, but the stock was renewing itself, and in
August 1609 Richard's second son was born: Alexander, the
name of the first Carew to inherit Antony. A year or so later
came a fourth daughter, Gertrude.

Richard was now nearly thirty, and finding his body over-
cold and moist, decided to try a nature cure with the celebrated rector of St Ewe, near Mevagissey. This was Hugh Atwell, who was then over eighty and had a prodigious reputation
throughout the West Country for his medical skill and generosity. In the *Survey* Carew had written a tribute to the old parson,
though the emphasis was on his bounty rather than on his
physic, which he treated with a mildly sceptical levity:

> Besides other parts of learning with which he hath been
> seasoned, he is not unseen in the theories of physic, and can out
> of them readily and probably discourse touching the nature
> and accidents of all diseases. Besides, his judgment in urines
> cometh little behind the skilfulest in that profession. Marry, his
> practice is somewhat strange, and varying from all others; for
> though now and then he use blood-letting, and do ordinarily
> minister . . . cordials of his own compounding (a point well fitting
> with my humour, as enabling nature, who best knoweth how to

work) yet mostly for all diseases he prescribeth milk, and very often milk and apples, a course deeply subject to the exception of the best esteemed practitioners; and such notwithstanding, as whereby either the virtue of the medicine, or the fortune of the physician, or the credulity of the patient, hath recovered sundry out of desperate and forlorn extremities.

Richard, remembering the excoriating purge that he had taken at Orleans ten years before, developed more gravely this theme of a vomit occasioned by deep drinking of milk. Atwell, he tells us, defended his practice quite logically as being 'nothing contrary to nature, but the abundance thereof, which filling the body did not strain the stomach so much as when the vomit came from it being empty, or having little in it, so endangering the breaking of veins; and that the milk turning into crud, would incorporate with the disease and so bring it away, when thin liquor could not, and that whiles it remained in the body before it came away, it rather gave a strengthening nourishment than any way weakened it, as other vomits use to do by their contrariety to natural food.' This was much to Richard's way of thinking, for he would have nothing to do with weakeners of nature, though he added somewhat contemptuously that Atwell might have learned this kind of physic: 'from sucking children, whom the infinite wisdom of God hath made by this means to avoid their diseases by casting up their milk when they could never express their griefs, nor their mothers know what to give them.'

So, 'drawn thereunto by the persuasion of my friends, who recommended his honesty, skilfulness and the gentleness of his physic,' Richard went to stay with the parson of St Ewe. All went well to begin with, 'for when being with him in his house, by feeding me often with warm milk and bread and some slight sweet nourishing things in it, I recovered my flesh and strength well again.' But 'continuing the same diet, and using milk instead of drink at my meal with my meat, it made me surfeit on the flesh which I did eat, and cast me into such a violent inflammation as that I was fain to go into the coolest air I could, and then continuing the same feeding upon warm milk and bread, the savour of all kind of flesh grew loathsome unto me. When I considered this, I thought there was no reason for me to hope to live, when my strength was so much abated as being near the age of thirty I could not live with such food as he did who was past fourscore. Therefore I went unto him, and told him that I perceived how I grew worse and worse with keeping the diet of filling myself with so much milk (for his ordinary word was 'keep full still'), and when I asked him what other course he would advise me to take, when I perceived by his uncertain answer that he knew not well how to direct me, I told him that I had long tried full-feeding for the recovery of my health, but now feeling that I rather impaired than amended thereby, I would see what good-fasting would do unto me.

'Whereupon, the day being calm and the sun shining warm, I rode softly abroad into the fields, and with the gentle exercise of my body, comfortable heat of the sun and not many hours' abstinence, my spirits exceedingly revived, and as I entered into his house I smelt cold veal; and whereas the savour of all flesh before was offensive unto me, that was then pleasing when I went unto him in his chamber. I told him how much I had been comforted by my being abroad, and seeing an empty urinal stand in the window of the chamber, I told him I would make water therein that he might observe my state, which when I had done and showed unto him, he said that the state of my body was as much amended as any man's could possibly be in so short a time, which made me mark the water a great deal the more diligently. By which it pleased God to make me conceive that when a body is overcome with coldness and moistness, the best way is to use abstinence.' As always, Richard was right, and able to show the expert just where he was wrong.

He was also right about Rawe Clyes, another professing physician of whom his father had written as one of the more notable curiosities of Cornwall:

The most professors of that science in this country . . . can better vouch practice for their warrant than warrant for their practice. Amongst these I reckon Rawe Clyes, a blacksmith by his occupation, and furnished with no more learning than is suitable to such a calling, who yet hath ministered physic for many years, with so often success and general applause that not only the homebred multitude believeth mightily in him, but even persons of the better calling resort to him from remote parts of the realm to make trial of his cunning by the hazard of their lives; and sundry, either upon just cause or to cloak their folly, report that they have reaped their errand's end at his hands.

But Richard knew even better: Clyes was something far worse than a charlatan; he was a fortune-teller, a conjurer, a calker, one in league with the Devil, like the woman whose eyes goggled in her head when he was a child. 'Once when a neighbour of mine, one Chark, had been with this calker to know what was become of his barge's sail that was stolen, the next time I saw him (because he had ever been kind unto me) I desired to talk with him, and told him I was very sorry he had been with the calker for his sail, for he must know the Devil was an enemy to mankind, and therefore would never do us any good except it were to make it a means to do us further mischief. And I wished him to report what he had done and never to do the like again, and to mark well, that though he had recovered his sail, within a twelvemonth he should find he should neither gain nor save by it.' One of Richard's own little failings was a weakness for fortune-telling, though, of course, not prompted by the Devil. 'When I talked with him, he would shake his breast with such violence as if he meant to break the bones thereof, and told me he was showed such sights as were able to kill the heart of any man, and was (as we say) never his own man after.

'And within two or three months after, having sold some sand in the country for ten shillings, and casting the wind and tide to serve well for his other barge that went with the sail that had been stolen, returning homewards singing, one of his acquaintance met him on the water and asked if he heard any news. He told him "No." Then replies the other, "Your barge is lost." When he asked how, he said Mr Porter's barge and his were turning upon the tide and neither of them would give way to the other, so his barge was stemmed and sunk in the river. So he lost barge, mast, sail, and all except the men, which it pleased God to preserve.'

This again was most satisfactory, but it was not the end of the affair, for: 'As I was telling these things to another, a third person that was by replied, "It sped better with me when I went to the calker for my horse, for I have him again." I answered, "So you might without his help. But tell me what it cost you." "Ten shillings to him," said he, "and ten shillings more in seeking; but I will not take four pounds for him." I replied, "Then cast your pennyworths too, and before the year comes to an end you shall find you shall neither gain nor save by it." About a fortnight after, he came hither again, and as soon as he saw me said: "Sir, you told me true about my horse." I never remembered I had spoken with him about any such thing, therefore asked, "What horse?" "The horse", said he, "I went to the calker for." "Why," said I, "the year is not yet out." " 'Tis true," said he, "but my horse fell into a gripe and then died." So he lost his horse, his charge and a fortnight's grass, and had not so much as one day's service of him after he sought him by his unlawful means.'

To go to calkers like Rawe Clyes out of idle curiosity was even more reprehensible than seeking their aid for the recovery of lost property. 'A gentleman of my acquaintance told me he went purposing to see a devil, but when the devil came to him he heard him only talk a few fustian terms, but could see nothing, and so returned merrily home, thinking with himself by the way what a fool he had been to go so far to such an ass to look for such wonders. With which speech of his, being extraordinarily moved, I suddenly told him he was bound more to thank God than he was aware of, for if he had had his desire it would have turned to his uttermost mischief. "Why," replies he, "he should have done me no harm." I answered, "I am not half so false a knave as the Devil, and yet if you'll allow me the power you will acknowledge the Devil hath, I would undertake to make your heart quake, if you were the stoutest man that ever went upon two legs, I would show you such sights." "I pray," said he, "what be these sights would make me so much afraid?" "You will grant", said I, "the Devil can make pictures of air, such as he pleases." "And what be those pictures," said he, "that be so terrible?" I said I would show him his own person committing all the sins he ever did since he was first born, with all the circumstances of time and place, and how many times God had offered him grace, how he had neglected it, how he had rejected it, with some part of the future course of his life, and how at last (as far as man could comprehend it) he himself would become a devil. Whereat he suddenly started with amazement, held up his hands and cried out, "O God! this is the fearfulest sight can be showed to any living man." I told him, "You must think then how the Devil himself would have dealt with you if he had had you to task." ' Nothing could be more agreeable than this snatching of souls from the burning.

In 1610 William Carnsew, youngest son of old William Carnsew, became Richard's uncle by marrying his aunt Anne Arundell. Anne was about Richard's age, but William was much older, for he had become a fellow of All Souls thirty years before, dividing his time between Oxford, London and Bokelly, where the three brothers and two sisters, 'not through any constraining necessity or constraintive vow, but on a voluntary choice, make their elder brother's mansion a college of single living and kind entertaining.' A great friend of Richard's father, Carnsew was a scholar with a keen sense of humour, who must have been amused by his earnest, puritanical nephew, and enjoyed pulling his leg, as when he told him the story of the Devil and the shoulder of mutton, a story that Richard solemnly recounted.

'I heard mine uncle William Carnsew (a gentleman of very excellent good parts) relate how, when he was in Oxford, one who was but too well acquainted with the Devil came to him, desiring his acquaintance and, to make himself the more esteemed, offered to show him what great things he could do by his art. When mine uncle objected that it was contrary to the will and word of God, he answered there were two sorts of conjuration: one servile, such as witches use who are made by the Devil to do what he lists, and the other imperial, which by the virtue of such words as he cannot resist makes him do what pleases those who have skill in that art. Whereunto mine uncle replied that he thought the Devil was a nimble knave, and might do pretty service if a man knew how to master him well.

'Whilst they were talking, one Mr Peter Green standing by began to tell him he was a mere impostor, and could do nothing but prate, which the conjurer taking with much indignity to have his skill so contemned, told him presently he could tell him at that instant what was done in any part of the world. Mr Green replied, "The devil thou canst!" Then he said, "You have a brother which is a soldier in France." He answered, "A hundred could tell that." He said further, "At this time your brother is going from such a place to such a place," which he truly named, "and he marches with a shoulder of mutton on his pike." Mr Green answered, "That is as true as the sea burns." Within three days after he met him again and told him, "This morning your brother is gone out upon service before such a place, and there is shot and slain." Within a while after this, over comes a soldier out of France unto Oxford, an acquaintance of Peter Green's, and meeting him there tells him, "I am very sorry for your brother's mishap, for," says he, "it was his ill fortune such a morning to go out upon service before such a place, and there to be shot and slain. But about three days before, your brother had gotten a shoulder of mutton which, when he could not tell how to carry, he put it upon his pike and make the best sport with it we ever had in our lives." After which news Peter Green shunned the meeting of him as he would have done the Devil himself, and feared him too much, as before he had contemned him.'

Thus Richard passed the first idyllic decade of the seventeenth century, with Bridget, his young family and natural history, his bees, orchards and birds, with gossip, Socratic arguings and the accumulation of unnatural stories. But it came tragically to an end in the spring of 1611. Bridget died in April, probably after child-birth, herself still little more than a child, for their fourth daughter, Gertrude, was born that year. Apparently his parents, and perhaps his children, were present at the harrowing scene: 'When she prepared herself for death, telling me she desired not to live any longer even for my sake nor for her children's sake, she said, "I leave them to God, who is able to provide for them without my care; but I desire to be with Christ." Then she earnestly requested me, if I saw a good opportunity, to marry again; whereunto, when I answered she should leave that to me as God should put it into my mind, she replied, "For God's sake do." And as she lived, so she died, for when I saw her drawing to everlasting life by the passage of death, we fell to prayer for her, and as long as any power remained in her hands during our prayers, she never missed to lift them up at the name of God, Jesus or Christ, and when they failed, she supplied it by the motion of her eyes, till with the end of her prayers she herself ended this mortal life.' Her last words were, "Lord, though thou killest me, yet will I put my trust in thee."

'And when she was dead I found in her pocket a prayer book, a true instruction for my poor remaining life, which she had collected out of a sermon she had read, and transcribed with her own hand, that by David's example we must never look for rest, but always prepare for new trials, each succeeding other in difficulty as well as in time, as the Scripture showeth us he did: first encountering a bear, then a lion, after that Goliath, and then Saul's persecutions, and after all this (though his love were excessive unto him) his most fair and wicked son Absolom's treason.' Poor Bridget! But another thirty years were to pass before the irony of this final ordeal became manifest.

'What a jewel I lost when she departed,' Richard wrote, 'any man may guess, but none can so truly value as myself,' and he put up a memorial on the arcade of the north aisle in Antony church: 'M.S. Brigidae, illustri Chudleighorum stirpe prognatae. . .'

> Sacred to the memory of Bridget, of the illustrious stock of Chudleigh, who by marriage became a member of the family of Carew of Antony. Devout, upright, decorous and the mother

of many children, she was, alas, suddenly taken by death in the middle of life.

Her husband Richard, to perpetuate his love and her deserts, set up this memorial.

She died 11 April 1611.

Of her children, she sent her son Nicholas before her to heaven, but left surviving her Alexander, Elizabeth, Martha, Mary and Gertrude.

The grief of Bridget's death almost carried Richard away too: 'After being so much weakened by the conflict I had with this piercing grief still prevailing against the best resistance I could make, one day having taken a little rest at noon, when I awaked, seeing both my hands look more like the dead than the living, I called my children unto me, and willed them to remember how God had already taken away their mother, and bade them look on my hands that they might see that I was not likely to tarry long after, and that therefore I wished them to take care to make the best use they could of the little time I was like to be with them, assuring them I was glad my task was so near at an end.' This exhibition of self-pity must have been a terrifying experience for those five children, the oldest of whom was only nine; yet it did Richard good, for his joy at the thought of his own approaching end was so great 'as thereby God restored me to my strength and health again, and prolonged mine unexpected life, and made it more pleasing than ever it was before. By her death I presently discovered how gently God had dealt with me in those things which before her loss seemed intolerable, but now I would have accounted a great happiness to have endured, so as I might have enjoyed her society whom I loved so dearly, and by whom I was no less dearly beloved. But God, who turns all things to the best to those that love and fear Him, converted this love I bare His creature to Him that was our Creator, and taught me so to withdraw mine affection from the world as, I hope, my heart shall never rest in it, but only on Him; by which I have received no diminution of any delight I enjoyed heretofore, but a far greater increase, so as I may confidently say, my greatest earthly loss became my greatest gain.'

5

The Widower

Bridget had implored Richard to marry again for the sake of her children, but inspired by her death, 'I began to take her task upon me, in doing my poor endeavour to breed those God left us to His knowledge and service, esteeming it the greatest good I could do for them'—unfortunate children!—'and myself too; for before this time my use was (after my private praying and reading of the Scripture) to employ myself awhile about something that in my age might do good to me and mine, and another while in reading, that I might be the better enabled both for the public and domestic duties.'

Not only did he take upon himself the function of a divine, however, but also, with his mistrust of doctors, that of a physician. Thus: 'Once my daughter Martha, being extreme sick, and as I feared in the pangs of death, my mother coming out to see her, said unto me, "Will you let her go on this fashion?" I answered, "If it please God to have her, I cannot keep her." My mother replied, "You have a water much commended for helping in such extremities," and bade me give her some of that, saying, "It may do good, if not, she can but die." Whereupon I did it, and she began to recover life and strength, and afterwards when she perceived how those pulls were coming upon her, called for a spoonful of that water, and by taking thereof, prevented them, and by God's mercy recovered her former health.' This is the only glimpse we have, either in the *Survey* or in Richard's *Memoirs*, of his mother; a capable, sensible woman, like a breath of fresh air in that febrile household.

The elixir with which Richard restored Martha, then about ten, was one that he had discovered in London in 1612 when his uncle George was ill. 'A little after my wife's decease, being at London with mine uncle Sir George Carew, when he lay sick, and but a little before he died, a minister very kindly brought unto him a glass of a water called a most precious water, and withal gave him a note to show the way how to make that water, which I then copied out, and have given many copies thereof to my friends, because in many extremities it hath done me very much good.' Yet, despite the precious water, Sir George died in November, leaving a fortune of £10,000, a widow Thomasin Godolphin, and the manuscript of his *Relation of the State of France*. Richard represented his father, who was too infirm to attend, at the funeral in St Margaret's, Westminster.

A few years later, apparently in 1617, he almost lost his only son, the eight-year-old Alexander. 'When mine eldest son fell sick on a Sunday at noon, of so violent a burning fever, being of the age of eight or nine years, and his flesh so scalded with the heat thereof that I could hardly suffer to touch it, and that he did not sweat, I knew this extreme heat followed some great cold which went before it. Whereupon I charged him to use as little moisture as possibly he could, and then took some cold water and washed his face, hands, back and feet, and allowed him the open air of the casement whiles he was awake. His heat was so great that when I washed his face with cold water, I saw it dry suddenly, and how the fume passed from thence as it goes from hot iron when it is poured thereon. Yet, I thank God, by this means only, though the violent heat continued three days in this force, in three days more he was perfectly well, though much of his flesh was therewith consumed away.

'When he was in the greatest extremity of this disease, an old, faithful and loving servant of this house came unto me and said, "Sir, what do you mean to do with your son? He is sicker than you are aware of." I answered I knew he was exceeding sick, and asked him what he would have me to do. He told me

I should send for a physician, and added, "Wherefore hath God made the physician, but to help in time of need?" I answered, "If I know how to save him, must I needs send for a physician to kill him?" He replied, " 'Tis well you will be ruled by nobody but by yourself, but when he shall be dead, nobody will be so sorry for it as yourself." Which speech grieved me extremely, because knowing what danger he was in, and assuring myself I used the best means to recover him, as I had found by trials in mine own person and other of my children many times before, I thought with myself with what extreme danger I was pressed on both sides, how I could answer it unto God if I used not the best means I might to save him, and how, if it should please God to take him from me, I should ever have it laid to my charge that I had wilfully cast him away. But I humbly thank God, it pleased Him to hear my prayers and to give a blessing to mine endeavours.'

However much we may be exasperated by Richard's obstinate self-sufficiency, we cannot but admire the courage, amounting almost to heroism, of his refusal to shift the responsibility on to the shoulders of another. The loss of Alexander would have been the cruellest blow of all, and his agony and devotion are reflected, graven rather, in his prose written twenty years later: 'His heat was so great that when I washed his face with cold water, I saw it dry suddenly, and how the fume passed from thence as it goes from hot iron when it is poured thereon.'

Richard's relations with his young family are also reflected in the numerous images evoked by memories of their childhood. Here is Richard taking his children for a walk: 'God never leaves us, though he sometime use us as we do our children when we lead them abroad and see them negligent in coming after us, gathering sticks and stones, and all the foolish toys they can see by the way, till having lost the sight of us they leave all and run and cry after us, and, for fear of the like, hold us fast as they can until some new thing make them forget what was past, and so they need our help again.' Here is the family in a bleak-morning, less coming-on disposition: 'We may with much pity look on all the blind and mad fools of the world, who like stubborn children refuse their desired breakfast because their bread is not buttered on the same side they would have it.' And here is Richard playing with young Alexander, and perhaps the girls as well: 'As men for sport do with little children, offering to wrestle with them, and falling when they see them use their poor force to prevail, and when they are down, desiring their help to get them up again.'

But the most charming picture of all is that of his youngest daughter, the seven-year-old Gertrude, and the figs, an incident that took place shortly after Alexander's illness. 'On a time, having bought figs, when I gave of them to my children I began with the youngest and gave her one, for which she returned me thanks, and then closely I gave two to each of the rest, and ended with one other to her who had the first, for which, imagining she had twice as many as the others, with great joy she took it. Which when the rest saw, they began to smile at the conceit they perceived she had, that her part was double to theirs; with which she presently entered into a jealousy that they had as many as herself, and when by my command they refused to show her what they had, her jealousy provoked her anger (for she was about seven years of age) and comes and lays at me with both her bee's fists. When I asked, "What's the matter you are so suddenly angry with me for that which but even now you gave me thanks?" she answered, "They have two apiece." I said, "Have you ever a jot the less for that?" "No," says she. "Why be you angry then?" "You have cozened me," says she, "for you made me make you two curtsies and thank you twice, when they did it but once."'

It is delightful, but one is chilled to find that the jest was merely an occasion for a moral, not for laughter, for Richard continues: 'At which her childish reason, when the rest began to laugh, I told them, we are all as foolish as she in greater matters, for when we receive many blessings from Almighty God, which of themselves are worthy more thanks than ever we could give, we are ready to undervalue them and repine at Him when we see others receive the like, whom in our corrupt judgment we esteem not so worthy as ourselves. I therefore willed them to take care not to commit the same fault they condemned in her.'

The episode introduces a section of Richard's *Memoirs* called *A Discourse Occasioned by Figs*. The date was about 1618, when England had been for many years at peace, though the Channel was infested with pirates who preyed on English shipping, which a neglected navy was quite unable to protect. Eastern Cornwall suffered severely from privateers based on Dunkirk, but even more formidable were the Muslim pirates from Morocco, who not only attacked merchantmen and fishing fleets but even raided the ports and carried off men, women and children to slavery. They snatched sixty from a church near Penzance, eighty from Looe, and when they raided Fowey one of their victims was Richard's niece, daughter of his brother John, 'the one-handed Carew'. Life along the Cornish coast was even more dangerous than it had been in the long Elizabethan years of the Spanish war, and Richard was one of the gentry responsible for the militia and defence of the Plymouth approaches. The danger occasioned a characteristic reflection, a delicious thrill at the anticipation of hardships that he was so unlikely to have to undergo.

'Within a while after, we had here a sudden alarm upon our coasts, upon which I received a command to make ready the foot company I had charge of; from which when I returned I began to think with myself how little I had considered the great blessing I had so long enjoyed by the great mercy of Almighty God in the continual peace wherein I lived all the days of my life here; having still plenty of things for myself and all mine, rising when I listed, going to bed when I pleased, quiet rest, warm lodging, without fear or danger: and how suddenly war would alter the case with me, in making me send away my children I knew not whither, to be out of danger, about whom I could not but be troubled, because I could not know how they did: and how I must endeavour to preserve my life by exposing it to all the hazards of war, shift for my food, and for my rest as I could catch it, and prepare myself to endure cold, heat, hunger, hardness, hurts, and death itself, into whose mouth I must put myself every hour. So as I began to think how glad I should be to recover but one week of such times as I had had many years, to be merry with my friends, come to my old ease, plenty and safety, the sweetness whereof I relished much the more perfectly because I saw how quickly I might lose them.

'While these things were in my mind, my hand, ere I was aware, was in my pocket where I had figs, and as I began to eat one of them I bethought me: he that planted the tree that bare these figs did it not of purpose for me, nor those who fetched them so far off never thought on me when they did it, yet God caused these He had ordained for my use by their means to be brought unto me, and their savour was pleasant unto me. And then methought there was no reason why I should not depend upon Him for all things else, Who daily gave me such tokens of His power and favour.

'And walking abroad with my children, desiring to frame them to the like confidence against all perils, telling them the invasion of our enemies was feared, I asked one of them whereof the best armour was to be made. I was answered, "Of iron." "Indeed," said I, "that yields the best matter to make armour," but then said to another, "Wherewith is the best armour made?" "With wit," says the other. Then I asked a third whether there were any other armour. I was answered there was an armour of wit by which we might get advantages of our enemies and save ourselves. All which armours I told them were to be used against our enemies and the surest of all was confidence in God Almighty, to dispose of all things for the best to those that love and fear Him. And this I called the Fig Armour, without which I would never wish them to go.'

One cannot help wondering what sort of man, what sort of women, this boy and these girls would grow up to be. It must have been with relief that they sometimes escaped from the moral hothouse of their home, where every innocent incident was barbed with a moral, to the healthier atmosphere of Antony

House and the company of their grandparents and young uncle Wymond.

Perhaps they stayed there when Richard was called away by his public duties, as in 1614, when he was one of the two representatives of the county in the Parliament of that year. One of the forty-two borough members was his boyhood friend John Pym, and another young John Eliot of Port Eliot, who represented his native borough of St Germans.

King James had already estranged both Puritans and Catholics, who had tried to blow him up, and he had treated his first Parliament to a long discourse on the authority of kings. 'The State of Monarchy,' he assured them, 'is the supremest thing upon earth: for Kings are not only God's Lieutenants upon earth, and sit upon God's throne, but even by God himself they are called Gods. . . Kings are justly called Gods, for they exercise a manner or resemblance of Divine power upon earth. . . As to dispute what God may do is blasphemy . . . so is it sedition in subjects to dispute what a King may do in the height of his power.' This was no way for a Scot to address the nobility and gentry of England, and the Doctrine of the Divine Right of Kings, on which the Stuart dynasty was to founder, so antagonized his Parliament that he dismissed it. The second Parliament of 1614, which Richard attended, was no more amenable, and after two months of wrangling it too was dissolved, and James decided to govern, like God, without the advice of his inferiors.

Richard, therefore, was not absent very long from home. We do not know what part, if any, he took in the angry debates in this Addled Parliament, but on his return he took up a new hobby, the breeding of civet cats, 'which I never could learn any man in Christendom ever had besides myself, and have seen almost incredible things in them: their strange manner of fighting, the extreme difficulty in taming of them, and their inevitable loss if they be but once too much contended with.' One of them lived for over three weeks with nothing more to eat than a daily spoonful of Devonshire whitepot, and another he showed to the King when he visited Plymouth. He had been

78

told about these strange animals, 'for he had never seen any of this kind before,' by Richard's kinsman, Sir Francis Carew of Beddington in Surrey, and apparently crossed the Tamar to see one. 'When he understood how I bred him here, and saw him to be so exceeding wild, he asked me how it could be. I answered, whosoever should pursue this task as I had done should find how much we are bound to thank God that so many creatures were tamed for us before we were born.' Richard and James had much in common, and no doubt Richard was among the first to buy *The Workes of the Most High and Mighty Prince Iames* when they were published in folio in 1616.

He had for some time been busy with another venture. In March 1612 he and his father jointly entered into an agreement with the parishioners of Sheviock 'touching the building of a keye at Port Wrickell', a fishing village four or five miles west of Antony. In his will Carew was to write, 'I have erected a kea at Portwreckle which I promised that the contributors of the parish should enjoy certain privileges,' and it is amusing to read Richard's version. However, as he lived in Sheviock parish until he inherited Antony, he may have been the prime mover in the making of this little quay, which is still there.

'Not long after the death of my wife'—Bridget, it will be remembered, had died in April 1611—'I was entreated by the bargemen of our parish to build them a quay, and advised by my friends the rather to do it, that mine employment therein might make me somewhat the less remember her loss; which work I was not unwilling to do, because I saw it likely to be a benefit to my neighbours, and I hoped thereby the better to enable myself to do good to my country in a larger measure if it pleased God to give me an opportunity.' It also had the advantage of supplying him with a conscript audience for his subtle Socratic dialectics and lay sermons.

'For the making of this quay I was to use many workmen, with whom, when I was talking a little before Easter, knowing their custom to prepare themselves devoutly for the forenoon, though they would be ready to forget it at the afternoon, I was desirous to speak somewhat unto them that might make them remember it after. But I thought if I should go by the ordinary way of exhortation, the first word would be ready to give them their fill'—how right he must have been!—'and their answer would be, I was a scholar and they none, and that it was therefore easy for me, but too hard for them; for prevention whereof, and to gain a diligent attention, I began in this manner:

' "The other day (said I) I met with a mad fellow who would needs have made a fool of me, and persuade me that the earth and sea did hang in the air (yet I could never make a feather hang there) and he offered to lay a wager that the sun (which shined then) should be witness to it. I said I had never heard the sun speak a word in my life, and I think if I had laid I had lost." Then they asked me merrily (thinking I had wit enough to escape the fool), "Who was it?" I answered, "It is no matter *who* it was, but I will tell you *how* it was. He asked me certain questions: first, whether I did not think the sun left air still between him and the earth and sea? I answered, I thought he did." And then I asked their opinion, and they told me they thought so too. "Then he asked me whether I thought not that he would keep one steady pace still, and never go faster nor softer for any man's pleasure, but how many miles he went one hour, so many he would go in another? I answered, I thought he did," and they said they thought so too. "And then he asked whether the sun would not be directly east at six in the morning? About this we had much reasoning before that point could be yielded, because we did not always see him there, yet upon examination it was granted too. Then that at noon he would be directly south, and at six at night directly west, which was likewise confessed. 'Then,' said he, 'I have got my wager.' When I asked how, 'Why,' says he, 'you confess that the sun in twelve hours goes from the east to the west by the south, and in twelve hours more will return thither again; then one of these ways he must go: either by the direct line from west to east, but that he cannot, for the direct line being shorter than the compass, the like pass would bring him sooner thither; or he must return by the south as he went forth, but that he cannot, because in the summer we see him before he comes to the east, and after he is past the west, and so of necessity he must descend as much under us at twelve o'clock at night as he mounts over us at twelve at noon, and so, compassing us round and leaving air alway between us, the air must needs compass us in too." And I bade them think on it, whether this God of ours had not an unmeasurable power, who made the light air on which a feather could not hang, to bear up the huge weight of the whole earth and sea.' Evidently Richard had not yet caught up with the discoveries of Copernicus and Galileo. Cosmography was not his strong point, and, had he known it, the truth was infinitely more wonderful than his pious imaginings.

'Another time, when some of our workmen were at dinner together, I began to be merry with one of them who took upon him more skill than he had, to make sport for others, and seeing him eating of meat, asked him, which was wiser, his head or his belly. He told me, his head. I said I looked for such an answer from him, and asked his reason. He said, because he could see, hear and understand with his head, and could not with his belly. Then I asked him again, whether that were not the the wisest that did the greatest wonders. "Yes," said he. "Then," said I, "look upon that spoonful of meat which thou holdest in thine hand, and see whether, with all the will thou hast in thy head, thou canst tell me how to turn it into flesh, blood and bone. Canst thou do it?" "No," he said. Then said I, "Put it into thy belly, and that will do it for thee." Then said I, "Look on it again, and see whether, with all the will thou hast in thine head, thou canst tell how to divide it into equal proportions for every part of thy body, to thine hands, thine eyes, thine ears, thy legs, and leave not so much as any one hair's part forgotten. Canst thou do it?" "No," he said. Then said I, "Put it into thy belly, and that will do it for thee." Then I bade him look on it once more, and see whether, with all the wit in his head, he could choose what would serve for nourishment, and keep that, and put away the rest. He answered, "No." "Then," said I, "put it into thy belly, and that will do it for thee." The conclusion was, that if God by these parts of our body we esteem most basely, work hourly so wonderfully for the continual maintenance of our lives, what is not the same God able to do when he shall please to use more excellent means?'

Thus Richard played Menenius to the labourers of Sheviock:

> The belly answer'd . . . 'Though all at once cannot
> See what I do deliver out to each,
> Yet I can make my audit up, that all
> From me do back receive the flour of all,
> And leave me but the bran'. What say you to't?

But he cannot have read the fable of the belly in *Coriolanus*, for the play was not then published. Perhaps he had marked and digested it in his father's copy of Camden's *Remains*, where Shakespeare himself had found it.

Perhaps, indeed, he had read the passage aloud to his father, for by 1612 Carew himself could no longer see the print. He had abused his sight by too much reading, poring over pages of Greek by the glimmer of tallow candles. Cataracts were beginning to thicken and close over his eyes, and by 1613 he was quite blind.

'When my father was blind, he made a little treatise to persuade others thus afflicted to suffer that great loss of one of our most precious senses at least with patience and equanimity, if they could not reach so far as to do it with true thankfulness. And as therein he made excellent use of his wit to prove this paradox, so did he really perform it in his practice, though I think no man could be more sensible of the want thereof, he ever delighted so much in reading. Three of us'—Richard himself, his mother Juliana, and daughter Elizabeth?—'continually supplying each other's weariness could not satisfy his hearing, for when he could see he alone used to do twice as much, for if he had none other hindrance, going [walking] or riding he would ever have a book and be reading. But from the latter he dissuaded me, because, though it pleased his mind, it did much hurt to his eyes.

'He ever took great delight in poetry, and often complained of their want of art therein, who when they took the pains to translate the Bible into our English tongue, put the psalms into such poor rhyme as they yet are sung in all our churches, by means whereof that exceeding comfortable Christian action of singing wants much in our language of the excellency it hath in others. And when a friend of his died, whose pleasing vein in that kind he much commended, and who had begun to amend some of them, my father bemoaned unto me, together with the loss of his friend, the loss of so good a work.' (The friend was probably his 'cousin', Michael Coswarth, who wrote *Certain Psalms in English Metre*, to which Carew contributed prefatory verses.) 'I told him we knew how far unsuitable to such an action the general course of the party's life was, and therefore could not tell whether God refused to take it from him; and seeing he was now dead, and the action so good, I said that he himself, who took such pleasure therein and had done so many other things in verse, should do well to undertake this, and that I thought God would accept it well at his hands. Then he began, as the most able use to do, to excuse his insufficiency for such a work. I desired him to try what he could do, whereupon, when he began to grow blind he also began this work, and continued and finished it in the two years he remained dark.'

We can imagine Richard, now aged thirty-two, fussing round his father, overwhelming him with pious exhortation and medical advice, experimenting with his precious water, his warming-stones and veronica juice ('I have heard that it hath cured the cataract, and a neighbour of mine told me that he recovered the sight of his eye when it was grown quite dark') and finally persuading him to submit to an oculist's needle. 'For God was so exceeding gracious unto me, as to make me a special instrument to persuade him to the cure of his eyes, and He made that man's hand to help him, who failed in his endeavour in the same kind for many others whom he could not cure, and gave my father his sight perfect, with the help of his block spectacles, in that eye first that he which undertook it, when he was doing of it even despaired to perform; and when he had done all, left him blind in that eye which he was very confident to cure. Yet after, without any further help of the oculist, God restored the sight thereof also, and continued it unto him about five years, even as long as he lived.

'And the first thing he spake of unto us after the removing of his cataracts was: "None of you knows how great a blessing God gives us by light and sight, but I who had now almost forgotten it by wanting of it continually two years together, when He removed my film the light appeared suddenly with such a glory (for the day was fair and the sun shined bright) that I thought with myself how much more glorious must that light be in which He dwelleth, Who hath made this natural light for His creatures." '

Perhaps it was to celebrate his recovery that Carew gave the dinner party at which Richard was present with some of his father's old friends and kinsmen: Sir Richard Edgcumbe, who had succeeded his father Peter at Mount Edgcumbe in 1607, Sir Richard Carnsew, the eldest of old William Carnsew's three sons, and Edmond Fortescue of Fallapit in Devon. They were all about the same age, sixty, and when the ladies had withdrawn and the wine flowed freely, talk turned naturally to the old Elizabethan days, the mining misadventures of Edgcumbe's and Carnsew's fathers, and the legendary activities of Burchard Cranach, *alias* Doctor Burcot.

Cranach was a German mining engineer, probably a Catholic refugee, who came to England in the reign of Mary, when he was granted a twenty-year patent to 'mine, melt and search for all manner of metals in any place'. By 1555 he was in Cornwall, where, like Dousterswivel in Scott's *Antiquary*, he practised on the credulity of Peter Edgcumbe and William Carnsew until he found medicine a more profitable profession, and in 1561 was naturalized and set up in London as a physician under the name of Doctor Burcot. 'This story', Richard writes, 'each of the parties before named told by several pieces, as if they had met on purpose to relate Burcot's life and death,' and we must imagine him, all ears, as he listens to his elderly kinsmen capping one another's stories and adding picturesque detail to an anecdote.

'This Burcot, when he came hither out of Germany, got ac-

quainted with mine uncle Peter Edgcumbe and with the old
Mr Carnsew, who addicted themselves but too much to adventure their certain means upon the uncertain hope of increasing
them by finding rich tin mines, which Burcot promised to
direct them where to find them, as indeed he did. But when he
had directed them where they should dig, after they had bestowed much labour and charge, and were come to the sight of
such plenty as they hoped the next day to make themselves
rich, that night there fell into their work so great a quantity of
loose earth and rubbish as they had no less to do to rid it than
they had at first to open it. Upon which, when they had again
bestowed more charge to come to it the second time, they were
again served as at the first, and forced to give it over for dear
at the last.'

Fortescue now takes up the story, and tells how his father was
nearly robbed of his inheritance by his rascally stepfather, who
sent him to Burcot with a sample of his water. 'In the meantime
the Doctor practised physic and did great cures. When my
cousin Fortescue's father was sent to him with his stepfather's
state (who had married his mother, an heiress, and he by profession a lawyer) he met one Parson Lark by the way, who told
him whither he was going, and how it was no marvel the
Doctor did strange things, "For," says the parson (who used a
familiar too, which he kept enclosed in the stone of a ring), "as
soon as you name the party to him he sees all the inward
parts of the sick man's body laid open as plainly before him as
we do the outward." When he came to Burcot, he asked for the
name of the party and said presently, "By God's pestilence, he
shall die." When Mr Fortescue told him that he knew his
stepfather must needs die, but desired his help that he might
recover now, he replied, "By God's pestilence, I tell thee he
shall die now. Thou thinkest he be thy friend; he be no thy
friend, thou shalt find it so. Thou meet a man upon the way
today, he no see me, I no see him; he know me well, I know
him well." At his return his stepfather died, and in his study
after his death he found a conveyance made ready for his
mother to seal, which his stepfather (the lawyer) had prepared,

to make her disinherit her own son and convey all her land to himself, if death had not speedily prevented it, when his stepson suspected no such matter, but esteemed him as his dearest friend, till he discovered this kind practice of his.'

The next story reads like a composite production of the three elder Richards: Carew, Edgcumbe and Carnsew. Sir William Mohun of Boconnoc was the father of Sir Reynold, young Richard's brother-in-law. Lord Hunsdon, a first cousin of Queen Elizabeth, was to become the patron of Shakespeare's company of actors, and Richard makes an error, for the date of the events related in this story is 1562, more than twenty years before he became Lord Chamberlain.

'Near that time this Burcot cured Sir William Mohun of a very dangerous sickness, which made him much talked of and more esteemed by my uncle Peter Edgcumbe, who when going to London about some business, having occasion to talk with the then Lord Chamberlain Hunsdon, he found him sick of such a disease as posed all the London physicians; whereupon he commended Burcot's skill he had shown upon Sir William Mohun, and said he thought if any man could cure his Lordship, Burcot was like to be the man. Whereupon my Lord of Hunsdon entreated my uncle, upon his return into Cornwall, where Burcot then was, to do him the kindness to send him up, as he did, and desired my grandfather to ride up with him to defend him from any abuse might happen to be offered unto him because he was a stranger. And so he went up with him to that purpose, and the old Mr Carnsew sent also with him an old and faithful servant of his house, called Roach, in colour to attend the Doctor, but indeed gave him a secret charge to have a diligent eye upon him, that from London he might not steal home into Germany before he had performed his promise concerning the mines.

'So when they came to London together he was by my grandfather brought to the Lord Chamberlain, whom in short time he cured, and was by him brought and commended for an excellent physician to Queen Elizabeth, with whom when he had talked he told her, "My liege, thou shalt have the pox." At which speech she was so exceedingly offended that she said presently, "Have away the knave out of my sight!" And within a while she fell extremely sick, so that none of her own physicians durst minister unto her, which danger of her life filled the Londoners' hearts and mouths with sorrow and lamentation, for she was (as she most justly deserved) wonderfully well beloved of them and all her good subjects.

'When she fell into so great danger by this sickness, as they much doubted her life, some about her wished that Burcot might be sent for, which she consented unto, and two of the Court with a spare horse were commanded to bring him to the Queen. When old Roach saw them, he imagined for what purpose they came, for he had heard report of the Queen's fearful sickness, and thereupon goes up to Burcot, who was then walking in his chamber, and told him how the Queen was very sick and had sent for him. But he grew into a great rage, and sware by his ordinary oath, "By God's pestilence! If she be sick, there let her die! Call me *knave* for my good will!" Which when Roach heard, he told him he forgot where he was, that she was his sovereign, that to save her life he ought willingly to lose his own, and if he could save his Princess's life and would not, he would surely (whatsoever became of him) make him pay for it with the loss of his own, therefore bade him resolve either to go unto her or to die presently. So down Roach goes to those which were sent, and tells them the Doctor would make him ready and come to them by and by, and then carries up his boots and his cassock, and lays them down before him, and drawing out his poniard bids him dispatch, for one way or other he should quickly go. Whereupon in a furious rage Burcot snatches up his cassock and his boots and puts them on, runs to his cupboard, catches a bottle of liquor he kept there, puts it up in his pocket, flings down over the stairs, mounts presently on horseback without so much as saluting the parties who were sent for him, posts to the Court, and comes thither a good while before the messengers could come after him.

'He was presently brought to the Queen, and as soon as he saw her, says, "Almost too late, my liege," causes a pallet to be made for her, calls for a remnant of scarlet, laps all her body in it, save one hand which he would have to be out, lays her before the fire, then gives her his bottle to drink of, which when she had tasted, he asked her how she liked it, when she answered, "Well, for we found it comfortable." Then he bade her drink more, all if she would, as she did, and a little after, looking on that hand which was out, seeing divers red spots rising thereon, asked him, "What is this, Mr Doctor?" " 'Tis the pox," says he. At which, when she complained, because she much loathed that disease, he replied, "By God's pestilence! Which is better, to have the pox in the hands, in the face and in the arse, or have them in the heart and kill the whole body?"

'Not long after, she recovered her health and strength, then calls for him and tells him, "Mr Doctor, you have deserved the spurs, therefore we will here give them unto you," and she delivers him a pair of golden spurs which had been her grandfather's, Henry the Seventh. And she said farther, "Think on some other matter wherein we may gratify you better and we will be ready to do it." Shortly after, being advised by some of our county of Cornwall to beg Winslade's lands, who was a little before condemned for high treason, he prefers a petition to the Queen to have these lands bestowed upon him. The Queen granted it, and signed it with her own hand, but when he sought to pass it by the old Lord Treasurer Burghley (for it must go through his hands before the grant could be made perfect), he, supposing land of a hundred pounds (for so much it came to) to be too great a reward, stops it and crosses it. With which denial of the Lord Treasurer, Burcot at the return to his lodging falls into an extreme rage, exclaims on the Queen and him, and says, "She Queen over him! and he deny me what she give me! No, he be King over her, me care not for it," and so in his fury cast it into the fire.' If we remember Burghley's part in the Duchy Suit, this countermanding of Burcot's reward has the authentic ring.

'After which time he practised physic in London, and there married a wife, to whom he was always very unwilling to spare any money, except it were to buy things at half price, which then he would do most readily. She therefore perceiving it, when she bought anything for him, would tell him it cost not half so much as in truth she paid for it; whereupon he would brag to his friends what pennyworths his wife bought him, and by this means she got what she listed from him.'

The Winslade episode is probably a contribution by Carew, who in the *Survey* had briefly told the story of how John Winslade of Tregarrick, near Looe, was executed as one of the leaders of the Prayer Book Rebellion of 1549, and forfeited his estates. The whimsical anecdote about Mrs Burcot is characteristic Carew, but it is Fortescue who makes an end of the egregious Doctor.

'A little before his end his familiar left him, and he dealt with a juggler called Feats (a man of the same trade, but one that used double juggling) to procure him a new familiar. Now Feats was a very cunning knave, who so mingled the help he had from his master with the subtle tricks of his own wit as made his wickedness the less suspected. He therefore told Burcot that for one hundred pounds in hand, and on condition that he would remain one whole hour in the same room where he would bring him, and not once step out of doors in that space, he should have what he asked. Whereunto having agreed, Feats left him in a chamber over a stable, whose planching was loose and the boards never joined together. Then under this room Feats set fire to wet hay and straw, and so fills the Doctor with smoke that either he must be choked or else get out, and so was well paid for his hundred pounds with which he meant to have bought a new devil. And not long after he died a beggar.'

As a matter of history, in 1577 Burcot was employed by Elizabeth in his original capacity, to test for gold the ore brought from Baffin Land, though he then complained of age and sickness. In September 1578 Susan Burcot was buried 'from Dr Burcott's' in St Clement Danes, and a month later the Recorder of London wrote to Burghley, 'Dr Burcott of St Clement Danes Churchyard is dead; I think of thought that he took for the death of a child of his.' Yet, although Fortescue's tall stories about Parson Lark and Feats are apocryphal, there is no reason to doubt the essential truth of the account of Queen Elizabeth's illness. In 1562 she so very nearly died of smallpox that Burghley called a meeting of the Privy Council to decide who should be her successor, and shortly after her recovery Elizabeth ordered payment of a hundred marks to 'Burchard Cronische, physician'. Apparently, therefore, it was Burcot who, when all was thought to be over, saved the Queen from death, and England from the miseries and dangers of a disputed succession (for who can say what would have been the fate of England if Elizabeth had died in 1562?), who was, in a manner responsible for the glories of the age of Shakespeare and Drake. It is to Richard that we owe this footnote to history, though he was himself more concerned with demonology than historical speculation, and his comment is: 'By this we may perceive the Devil never does good to any who have to do with him or any of his wicked limbs. For the mines, the adventurers had only the sight of a rich lode for their great charge, which the Devil knew before the beginning would so come to pass; for the diseases he cured, I shrewdly suspect he procured them by the secret help of his master, under hope of a great reward which he proposed to deceive him of at last, when he thought himself most sure of it.'

Apparently he saw nothing funny in these outrageous stories, but sat solemnly at the table meditating on the devilish wiles employed by Burcot. He was particularly interested in Feats. It is improbable that he ever read anything so frivolous as *The Merry Conceited Jests of George Peele*, but if he had come across this collection of tales about the riotous Elizabethan dramatist, long since dead, he might have found the story of George and the Barber:

> Anthony the Barber . . . therefore determined to come to London to seeke out George Peele, which by the meanes of a kinsman that Anthony Nit had in London, his name was Cuts or Feats, a Fellow that had good skill in tricks on the Cards, and hee was well acquainted with the place where Georges common abode was: and for kindred sake he directed the Barber where he should have him, which was at a blinde Alehouse in Sea-cole Lane. . . .

Whether Richard had ever heard of Feats or not, he pressed his cousin Fortescue to tell him more, and the elderly wag, with a glance, we may imagine, at the tense young man across the table, obliged.

'This Feats had many tricks to delude men by, which he would afterwards explain how he did them, so that what he did indeed by the Devil might be taken to be but a pleasant kind of cozening. Now, three things the same gentleman, my cousin Fortescue, told me he saw him do, two of which seem strange, but the third I cannot conceive how any man can do it but by the help of a spirit. The first was, when this Feats, dining at a table among divers knights and gentlemen, sat at the lower end of the table by one Mr Powell, who during the meal made himself very merry with Feats's precious nose and the rubies of his face, for he loved good liquor and carried these tokens thereof.' Another Bardolph. Evidently Fortescue knew his *Henry IV*. 'When the meal was ended, Feats, to make sport, called for a dish of nuts, bade one of the knights think on some card, and asked another whether he would have the name of the card so thought on to be written in red letters or black. He said red. Then he bade him take out a nut and crack it, which having done, within the hud which contains the kernel was found a little roll of parchment curiously folded, and therein the seven of spades written in fine roman letters, which was indeed the card the first knight thought on. Then he turned to Mr Powell and said, "You have taken your pleasure on me this meal, yet you shall see I will do something for you." So he bade another think on a card, and then told Mr Powell to take a nut and crack it, which when he did, such filthy black stinking stuff flew thence into his mouth and about his face as he could hardly in half an hour get it away. After which time Mr Powell held Feats in as great admiration as before he had done in contempt, and would often bestow wine on him.

'Now, once when my cousin Fortescue and Feats were to-gether in Wells (if I mistake not the name of the place), meeting this Mr Powell, Feats told him, "You have done me many courtesies, and if you will bestow a quart of wine on this

gentleman and me, I will requite all your former kindnesses."
Mr Powell agreed, so into the tavern they go, and Feats calls
for the chamberlain and asks him how many maids there were
in the house. He named him three, A, B, C. Then he bids him
bring three knives and a basin of water. When he was gone, he
takes a root out of his pocket, which seemed to be a furze root,
names each knife by one of the maid's names, and tells Mr
Powell he would teach him a trick to know whether anyone he
meant to marry were a maid or no. Then he whets the knives
upon the root and puts them into water, and says to the knife
which he called A, "If A be a maid, get up presently." Up flies
the knife and sticks in a beam of the roof. Then says he to the
knife called B, "If B be a maid, get thou up too." Then up
mounts that knife and sticks in the haft of th' other. Then calls
he upon C, if C were a maid, to follow her fellows. But that
knife was deaf and would not stir. Whereupon Feats calls again
to the chamberlain, and seems to fall out with him for saying
there were three maids in the house. The chamberlain tells
him again, so there be. Feats begins to chide him for offering to
maintain such a lie before him, and says he knew A and B were
maids, but C was none. The chamberlain answers, "The truth
is, sir, she had a young son some three months since, but being
my fellow servant, it was reason I should conceal it and speak
the best of her," and he desired them to do so for the credit of
the house. Whereupon Mr Powell agrees to buy this root of
Feats, which he saw to be of such proof, and pays him forty
shillings for it. And I think he might have tried all the maids in
Christendom before he should make his knife leap as the two
first did.

'Another time when Feats, my cousin Fortescue and others
were in company, he would needs have one of them to think on
a card, and have another to name the card. When he answered
he could not tell what card it should be, Feats replied, "Any
card which comes first into your mind." Then suddenly, as by
the shortest puff of breath, the name of the ace of hearts was
buzzed into his ear, and he said he could not tell what card it
should be if not the ace of hearts, which was indeed the very

card the other had thought. Now this kind of instruction passes my capacity, for one man by any natural means to give to another in this sort.'

Again one cannot help wondering what sort of effect this humourless, credulous father would have on the young children whose upbringing he had taken entirely upon himself; and soon they were to be deprived of the salutary influence of their grandfather. Carew, 'approaching daily through increase of years and infirmities to the period of his life', made his will in April 1619, when he was nearly sixty-four, and revised it in June of the following year, probably after the death of his youngest and only remaining daughter, Anne. She was only twenty-two. She had married Francis Godolphin of Treveneague, one of the overseers of the will, the others being Carew's second son, John, and his brothers-in-law, William Carnsew and John St Aubyn, a Puritan, like Godolphin. After making provision for his wife Juliana and four younger sons, he appointed Richard his sole executor and left him all his lands, patronages, woods, goods, leases and chattels. Four months later, at the beginning of winter, he died.

'God gave him such an end as he often told me he desired; for he would say he would willingly be sick a little before he died, that he might learn thereby the better to leave the world. And so he was; for the Saturday morning which was before the Monday on which he departed, when he came down from his chamber he told me, "This last night hath been with me as the first was of my last great sickness; I think I have turned a thousand times in my bed." So he had his visitation according to his desire. He likewise often told me, when he came to die he should be very loth to see and hear the lamentations of his wife and children, lest they might thereby trouble his mind, which at all times he held most meet, but then most especially necessary, to be fixed on God. Neither would he have them to expect exhortations from him, but that they should remember what he had from time to time persuaded them to when he was in health. Neither, if it so pleased God, would he be long in the passage.

'All which came so to pass; for the third day after his sickness, when we all little thought he had been so near his end, that morning he rose out of his bed and came down into the hall, and sate there a good while among his company, and from thence about three of the clock went up into his study. And there in the remotest place thereof, being at his prayers, as we guessed by divers circumstances (his usual hour being come, and having before set aside his hat), and as we think being on his knees, for they were folded under him, he fell down and died. And after he was dead he yet retained that natural cheerful countenance he ever showed his friends whiles he was alive. And after his death I found these verses written with his own hand, among the papers he had in the pocket of his hose, and I think they were the last he ever made:

> Full thirteen fives of years I toyling have o'repast
> and in the fowerteenth weary'd entred am at last:
> Whiles Rocks, Sands, Stormes & leaks to take my
>   barque away
> by dangers, sickness, troubles, sorrows did essay:
> And yet arrived I am not at the port of death,
> the Port to everlasting life that openeth.
> My time uncertain, certain Lord, long cannot be,
> what's best to mee's unknown, and only known to thee.
> O! by repentance & amendment grant that I
> may live still in thy fear, & in thy favour dye.'

In his will he had asked to be buried 'in Antony Church in the aisle where I sit, if I happen to die within a day's journey of that place, and within four and twenty hours of my decease, without mourning garments.' There, on November 7th, he was buried, and on the wall of the north aisle, facing his memorial to Bridget, Richard set up an unimpressive slate slab adorned with a tribute in his not over-accurate Latin: 'inivriarvm benificiis placidiss. . .'

A most peaceful man, who repaid injuries with kindness, most versed in books, and a most distinguished author of books, who ever deserved very well of his prince and country for his constant and faithful service. Of the learned, the poor and oppressed a most kindly supporter, who, having passed the span of 65 years well and happily, in the midst of his customary private daily prayers to God most good and great, in his library peacefully fell asleep in Christ on 6 Nov. 1620.

His son Richard Carew with tears set up this memorial to his most well deserving father out of dutiful affection. . .

Alexander was only eleven when his grandfather died.

6

Remarriage

'When I followed my father's corpse to his funeral, I saw so plain a copy of the sentence of my own death written by his, from whom I had my life, that it was even a wonder how I could outlive him; and I thought how exceeding glad I should be if it were possible to converse but one week again with such a father.' So, full of pious reflections, though not without a certain satisfaction, the widower of forty moved into Antony House: 'When I returned from the funeral to his house in which I now dwell, I thought with myself what especial favour God had done unto me in ordaining me to be the only man who should succeed him in his house and estate.'

He soon found further consolation in the management of his patrimony, and his health was, as ever, a not altogether unwelcome distraction. 'A little after the decease of my father, when I rode about my business to prepare for the finding of the office by which I must show by what tenures I held his land, as I rode over an open down I felt a general cold over all my body, which I regarded not, because it was little, and my way short. But by this neglect it gained so much upon my natural heat that it forced me to seek outward heats by stones heat by the fire, covered with woollen clothes, and to fast for three days together from meat and drink, which enabled me to get some heat and strength again.'

This ride in the early winter of 1620 taught him a lesson. 'This extreme cold in the bottom of the belly and members, which the tailors' foolish fashion in making breeches too deep in the seat, with the motion of the horse making them to blow like bellows on those parts, hinder the retention of water and much increase the pain of wind; and since that time I have taken special care to have my clothes so made as I might be sure to keep those parts of the body very warm.'

It was just as well, for soon after Christmas he was returned as one of the members for Mitchell in the Parliament that James had at last been compelled to call. So, early in January 1621 Richard, in his unfashionably tight breeches and, we may be sure, several layers of winter woollens inside them, joined the cavalcade of Cornish and Devonshire gentlemen on their long ride up to Westminster. Youthful oddity and prejudice had now become middle-aged eccentricity, much to the amusement, no doubt, of his companions. A generation later Thomas Fuller was to write of Carew in his *Worthies of Cornwall*: 'I know not whether he or his Son first brought up the use of *gambadoes*, much worne in the West, whereby, whilest one rides on horseback, his leggs are in a coach, clean and warme, in those dirty Countries.' We may be sure it was the son, and that he rode to London that winter with his legs inside those long boots attached to the saddle, instead of stirrups.

'After the forementioned cold over all my body, with a very spare and temperate diet and help of warming my drink, I adventured to take a London journey from my house to ride up to the Parliament, because I was then of the House. Travelling this journey in the company of divers gentlemen, one of them took exceptions to my diet when he observed how I called still for the newest drink I could get, and said unto me, "You complain how you are much troubled with wind, for your new drink will breed it exceedingly, and kill you." I answered, "If it does so, I hurt nobody but myself." He bade me ask any physician's opinion in England, and he would tell me so. Now, when I had found by many years' experience how nourishing new drink was unto me, and how stale drink, though it pleased my taste very well, yet bred much gravel in my body, and instead of filling my veins with blood, it filled them with a windy scalding water and weakened my heart, I thought I had little

reason upon his vain affirmation to change the course I had
found far more profitable for my health. Within a few days
after, the same gentleman came unto me again and said unto
me, "Sir, I shall intreat you not to take that offensively which I
spake when I sought to dissuade you from your new drink, because I hoped it would be for your good, and did it out of my
love unto you. But since continuing in your company, and seeing it do well with you, I adventured to taste of your cup—I
must confess, fearfully at the first—but then liking the taste
thereof and finding no harm come after it, I have been bolder
to use it, and perceive that it agrees better with my body than
the staler drink which I used before." I answered him, "Then
you know now what a wise man I should have been to have
left it upon your dissuasion." ' And so, chatting about wind and
gravel, stranguries and ruptures, Richard enlivened his
journey, and reached London in better health than when he
left home.

It was seven years since he had attended the short-lived
Addled Parliament, and for seven years James had managed
without the help of his Commons, raising money by the sale of
honours and monopolies, or simply by asking his subjects for
'benevolences'. The real ruler of England was his handsome
young favourite the Duke of Buckingham, with whom Sir
Richard Robartes, busy with the building of his great house of
Lanhydrock, was negotiating for a peerage that was to cost him
some £30,000. By 1620, however, James was in need of money
on a larger scale, for the Thirty Years' War of religion had
broken out in Germany, and his Protestant son-in-law, the
Elector Frederick, had been driven out of his principality on
the Rhine by the Spaniards. The Commons had no objection to
voting supplies in support of Frederick and the Protestants, but
first they turned their attention to the dubious ways in which
James had been raising money, and found a scapegoat in Lord
Chancellor Bacon. The member for Liskeard, Sir Edward
Coke, former Chief Justice, led the attack on Bacon, who, im-
peached by the Commons before the Lords, confessed that he
had been guilty of corruption, and was disgraced.

The Commons then turned to foreign affairs, bitterly assailing James's cherished policy of ending religious strife by marrying his son Prince Charles to a Spanish princess, and they sent a petition that he should marry a Protestant. James angrily told them to mind their own business, to which the Commons replied by entering in the Journals of the House a protestation of their right to debate all subjects that concerned the government of the country, foreign as well as domestic. James sent for the book, tore out the offending page, dismissed Parliament, and arrested some of the members responsible for the protestation. John Pym was one of these 'ill-tempered spirits'.

It is improbable that the member for Mitchell was another, for his only reference to these exciting events is: 'My continual sitting still about the business of the House, and want of fresh air and exercise, brought a very great cough upon me.' He does, however, develop this theme: 'When a friend of mine, one Mr Alexander Maynard, a counsellor-at-law, heard me much troubled therewith, he told me he had had the like, and that a client of his, a skilful physician unto the judges, had quickly cured him, and he thought, if I would use his help, he would soon free me from that disease. I thanked him, and said I took the cough to be hereditary, because my father was continually subject unto it during his life, yet I intreated him to ask the physician to come unto me. So having saved my water, when I showed it unto him, I prayed him to give me leave to acquaint him with the constitution of my body, and by what means I had recovered divers coughs and other like diseases, and how ill my body was able to brook ordinary physic, and that before I would receive it I should like to know how it would work, and how it should help me, for that I was very loth to be drenched like an ox or an ass with I know not what. When I had told him these things, I said, "Now, if you can show me any course by which I shall be likely to recover my health with more ease, speed or certainty, I will pay you and thank you for it too; if not, I will pay you for your pains, and thank you for your good will." He answered me, "I thank you with all my heart, sir, that you have dealt thus with me, for had I given you such physic as we usually give to men in your case, I had killed you; and if you can by such means as you told me, cure a body so far overgone with raw and rough humours as, by your water, yours seems to be—" I said I knew it to be rather more than less than he imagined, and he farther said unto me that, if I would be advised by him, I should take physic of no man, for that he thought no physician in England could prescribe me so good a course as myself observed.' All of which was again most satisfactory. 'So I paid him, and thanked him too.'

James dismissed his Parliament at the beginning of 1622, so that Richard was back at Antony by the end of January, But his journey had not been wasted. He had devoted the last ten years to the upbringing of his children, but now that he was a man of the first consequence in the county he felt the need of a wife to help him with his social duties. He was not a man to act rashly, so on his journey to London he took the opportunity of talking to one of his companions, Robert Rolle of Heanton in Devonshire, about his daughter Grace, and by the time they were back in Devonshire a marriage agreement had been arranged. Grace was to have a portion of £2,000—another marriage had its financial advantages—in return for which Richard assured her a jointure of £240 after the death of his mother Juliana, and soon after his return they were married.

Grace was barely seventeen, younger than Richard's eldest daughter Elizabeth, now twenty, and recently married to William Pearse, and she would be more of a playmate than a mother for Gertrude and Alexander, aged twelve and thirteen. Yet they were soon to have another brother, for before the end of the year John was born, first of the four sons who formed Richard's second family. He tells us nothing about Grace, and the only mention of any of her children is a parenthetic reference to John. 'One of our neighbours being grown so weak in her childbed that her speech and her sight failed her, one entreated me to have some of my precious water to give unto her. This they did by opening her mouth with a key, and by pouring in two or three spoonfuls, which when they did she knew it not, but within a while opened her eyes, and when they asked her whether she perceived anything, she said she felt a thing hot at her heart, and so recovered. And since that time she hath nursed my son John for me.'

James I died unhonoured in 1625, and was succeeded by his son Charles, a young man of twenty-four, as much under the influence of Buckingham as his father had been. The reign began on a note of popularity, for Charles and his favourite had abandoned the Spanish marriage and roused patriotic feeling by involving the country in a Spanish war instead; but goodwill was dissipated when the King married Henrietta Maria of France at the price of granting toleration to Catholics in England and a promise to help in the suppression of the French Protestants. War gave Parliament a chance to assert itself, for the King needed money for its prosecution, and when it met in 1625 Pym led an attack on Buckingham and a campaign for the enforcement of the laws against Catholics. After two months of wrangling Charles dissolved Parliament, and an expedition that was intended to repeat the triumphs of Elizabeth's reign was sent against Cadiz. But the raid was one of the most humiliating failures in our history, a humiliation of which Richard must have been well aware, for the expedition set out from and returned to Plymouth. Charles was now even more urgently in need of money, but when he called a Parliament at the beginning of 1626 Sir John Eliot of St Germans and John Pym led the Commons, which included Francis Rous and Richard's brothers-in-law, Henry and John Rolle, in the impeachment of Buckingham. To save his friend the King once more dismissed his Parliament, then, as if the war with Spain were not enough, fatuously allowed England to drift into war with France as well. Buckingham himself commanded an expedition to relieve the Huguenots of La Rochelle, a venture as disastrous as the Cadiz raid, and he returned with less than half the force with which he had embarked.

Meanwhile, to finance the war Charles had resorted to a forced loan. Many, including Eliot and John Rolle, refused to pay, and the Cornish, whose ports were full of disabled sailors and soldiers, particularly resented this arbitrary way of raising money. The county was supposed to pay £2,000, but the justices reported that the wealthier gentlemen 'were not able to give in that manner', though ready to contribute 'in a Parliamentary way', and a number of them were imprisoned. Money could not be wrung out of the English in this fashion, and as Charles and Buckingham insisted on prolonging the war, another Parliament had to be called to pay for it.

The Parliament of 1628 brought matters to a head. Under the leadership of Eliot and Pym the Commons forced Charles to accept the Petition of Right, which declared illegal all forms of taxation without the consent of Parliament, and the imprisonment of any subject without cause shown. They then proceeded to attack Buckingham, who was, however, to the exultation of the nation, assassinated, and the second expedition to Rochelle had to sail without him. The fleet mutinied when they saw the well-equipped enemy opposing them, and passively watched their Huguenot allies surrender to the French Catholics. A country's arms and honour could scarcely sink lower than that. The Commons, now becoming predominantly Puritan, then turned their attention to the new High Churchmen, the King's friends who, led by Bishop Laud, supported his despotic actions; but Charles had had enough, and decided to manage without Parliaments. He withdrew from the war on the continent, but before he could dismiss the Commons they passed three Resolutions, declaring that anyone who introduced innovations in religion, or advised or paid taxes without the consent of Parliament, was 'a betrayer of the liberty of England, and an enemy to the same'. Ignoring the Petition of Right, Charles imprisoned the members who were mainly responsible. One of them was Eliot, and another William Strode, a 'cousin' of Richard's.

This was the state of the nation when Richard began, or shortly after he began, to write his *Memoirs* in the summer of 1628: the gentry, the leaders of the people, brought almost to the verge of rebellion by the King's restriction of their liberties and his Anglo-Catholic sympathies, the country's prestige sunk so low that she was the laughing-stock of Europe. He was old

enough to remember the proud position that England held in
the last decade of Elizabeth's reign, and though he mentions no
names or specific events there is many a sigh at the country's
degeneracy. This he characteristically attributes to a decline of
religion, apparently a glance at the King's High Church principles and lack of Puritan fervour. 'Our prosperity hath so
much weakened Christianity as we have need of a Joseph to
renew the broken covenant between God and us, for our lives
and professions are almost clean contrary to one another. But
my hope and prayer to Almighty God is that He will be
pleased to make our religious King truly to know it, and duly
to reform it.' And he adds the dubious assurance that amounts
almost to a warning. 'And then I doubt not but he shall easily
find as many brave servants as ever prince had to make him
famous here and happy for ever after.' Later he returns to this
theme of material prosperity, the 'affluent society' of the day,
with a quotation from his father: 'poverty breeds peace, peace
breeds plenty, plenty breeds pride, pride breeds dissension,
dissension breeds wars, wars breed poverty.' Yet he was uneasy
and a little bewildered, for it was no longer as simple as in his
father's day: 'Now we grow poorer and prouder than ever we
were, for surely our sins have made us all sick and fall before
our enemies, so as our nation is become a scorn to our neighbours.'

Political allusions are few. Possibly he was thinking of Charles
I when he wrote: 'Great princes do not all employ money so
well, and as long as more may be had it never seems enough.'
Certainly he was thinking in terms of forced loans and the
Petition of Right in the passage: 'We have the whole power of
the King and kingdom to maintain the freedom of our persons,
and right to our goods and lands against any who by violence
would oppress us or take them from us. And if in these latter
times we find not such exact observation thereof as was used in
our fathers' days, yet it hath made no greater alteration than
the great mountains do in the general plains of the earth,
which though they seem to those who are near them to be of
huge and horrible quantity and height, yet show as nothing

when considered as they lie in the body of the earth.' The conclusion is revealing: in other words, the Commons are making
much ado about little, and even his reference to the iniquitous
billeting of soldiers in private houses is mildly phrased: 'We in
England have not only sufficient corn for ourselves but good
store to spare to others, so as when the army was maintained by
us, if we had had our promised pay, we might reasonably well
have borne it.' 'If we had had our promised pay!' This is not
the language of Pym and Eliot, languishing in the Tower:
'Upon this dispute not alone our lands and goods are engaged,
but all that we call ours. These rights, these privileges, which
made our fathers freemen, are in question.' For Richard the
fault lay not so much in the King as in the sinfulness of his
people, which had enforced God a little to overshadow the
sunshine of his blessings, and all might be restored by hearty
prayers and true repentance.

We do not know what Alexander thought. Now nearly nineteen, he was admitted to the Middle Temple in March 1628,
the month in which this historic Parliament met, and would
inevitably be caught up in the excitement of that critical year
of the Petition of Right. And the Inns of Court were one of the
chief centres of resistance to royal tyranny.

Although Richard was a Puritan, he was also a Royalist, at
least at the time of writing his book, for were not the Carews
themselves 'descended from the royal race'? And he begins
with a prayer that he and his family 'may ever express in all
things an extraordinary love to our princes, inasmuch as we
have more than ordinary cause,' and three years later concludes
with an affirmation of his belief in the Divine Right of Kings—
'Princes hold their crowns immediately by the Grace of God'—
and a supplication that English kings may all maintain their
estates in peace, the good will of their Parliaments, and die in
their beds. There can be few prayers that have so emphatically
been denied in all their detail.

7

Reflections

Richard's book begins with a section called 'Particulars concerning mine own Person.' 'Having this day finished forty-eight full years of my journey towards death, methought it was very fit for me to look about and consider what I have passed, that I may the better keep my way in the time that is to come.' And he considers how fearfully and wonderfully made he is, the germ of his substance having been in his parents' bodies, 'and how little that was compared to the measure of their persons, and how very much that very little was lessened as I went back to my grandfathers and grandmothers, and on from them to their parents' generations, my particular still decreasing as I found their number increasing, which in twenty ascents will amount to no less than 1,048,574.' (He conscientiously sets down his calculation in the margin, 2, 4, 8, 16 . . . , but makes an error in his addition, though a mistake of two in a million is not very serious.) 'And if any of this multitude had failed by the general calamities of the world or their own mishaps, I had missed the chance of my being.' It is certainly a thought to stagger the imagination, this gradual distillation of our essence through countless generations of our ancestors, until the converging sources are reduced to two, which by their union are finally concentrated in ourselves. Richard was full of wonder at the marvels of creation, though rarely as metaphysically imaginative as this.

Evidently he had been doing some genealogical research, for he tells us, rather surprisingly, that 'by my mother's race'—the Arundells of Trerice, or perhaps the Coswarths—'I find myself descended from the loins of Abraham, Isaac and Jacob, to whose posterity God himself promised continuance and special favour.' This, no doubt, was one reason why he considered himself one of the elect, and accounts for his fondness for the Old Testament, to the characters in which he so frequently refers: Moses, Abraham, Noah, Joshua, and particularly Adam, the ultimate source of his being. And, whether consciously or unconsciously, the Bible was the model for his prose. Too often it is inflated and diffuse, but he can write with vivid brevity—'a great bay at full sea upon the top of a spring tide'—and occasionally he coins an exquisite phrase: 'All the bewitching beauty of the world', which might be a line from a Shakespeare sonnet, but more often the rhythms and harmonies are those of the then recently published Authorised Version:

> Methusaleh's great age was in the end consumed by the minutes of time; and does not the sun run as fast now as he did in his days, and does not every inch he goes carry away a piece of the little time our lives last?
> We order our lives so, as if they should continue here for ever; and verily indeed, only the sons of God by grace expect a dissolution with royal fear and trembling for their great advancement.

As we should expect, his other principal references are to animals; and hawks, harts, hares, worms, snails, moles, dogfish, elephants and swallows all play their parts in his argument and narrative. Then there was the thurlepole, or whale, which a neighbour of his, thinking it to be a tunny, killed with a knife as it lay quietly as a piece of timber in the river below his house. 'But when I saw a great hole in the hinder part of the head, I conceived it to be a thurlepole, and viewing the body I observed two natural slits it had in the belly, which because I was desirous to know for what they served, I opened them a little, and presently saw two pretty little teats to give her young ones suck with.'

His sympathy with animals led him almost to an intuitive perception of an evolutionary process: 'God proceeds in his works by such degrees from one creature to another so like it as we can find no difference between them. So see we some stones laid in such sandy circles as we cannot tell where the stone begins, neither whether they have not in time increased their stony matter of it, as we see trees and plants increase their own bodies out of the earth; so do some growing things come so near the living that we cannot perfectly tell of which sort they are. . . So come baboons so near men in shape that the Indians have an opinion they can speak, but will not, for fear the Spaniards should make slaves of them.'

Monkeys fascinated him, and he has a story not unlike that of 'the famous ape' in *Hamlet*, which, to see what would happen, crept into a basket and broke its neck: 'The ape, who seeing a piece of great ordnance to be shot off, when the company were gone, took the linstock which was left with the match on fire in it, got upon the piece near the mouth and reached therewith to the touchhole, and as soon as he saw it fire, suddenly clapped his head to the mouth to see what would come from thence, and so was presently torn in pieces.'

Most of his stories point a moral, and the spider, of course is the perfect emblem of the Devil. 'The old serpent deals with the wicked as I saw an old spider deal with a strong fly, which, when he perceived to be entangled in his work, did not run upon him presently to suck out his life, but fetched new matter out of his body and wound it five or six times about him till he left him no power to stir; and then, when he was sure he could never escape, fell upon him and killed him. So that old and subtile enemy of mankind, when he hath once gotten the hearts of wicked people into his secret snares, does not by and by fall upon them, but ties them easily faster with more and more sins, till they have lost all the power to resist him.'

In Virginia, he was told, the Devil appears to the natives in visible shape, answering to the name of Tanto, and cruelly tormenting them if they refuse to obey him. Apparently their God behaved in much the same manner, a circumstance that led Richard to consider the blessings of living in England in the reign of Charles I. Even the poorest Cornish labourers expect meat at least three times a week, but the wretched Virginians, tormented by Tanto and beaten by their God, are reduced to eating a surfeit of fish, which 'so alters their complexions that they look almost as white and pale as the fishes themselves.' (It all sounds very much like *The Tempest*: poor Caliban, his god Setebos and ancient and fishlike smell, tormented by Prospero's art.) He contrasts 'their old Adam's fashion in covering their nakedness with skins' with the Englishman's 'clothes of all sorts' (though not without a thrust at foolish fashions) 'and not only clothes for ourselves, but for our horses, and for our cold walls to keep them warm, and those not of the meanest price neither.' He shudders at the thought of the squalor of a native hovel, and thinks of the comforts of Antony House: 'Such soft and warm beds, such pleasant orchards, gardens and walks, such service of creatures for our ease, making the oxen to plough for us, the horses to travel our journeys for us while we sit still on their backs, and to draw us in wagons and coaches, such store of men and women servants ready to do what we desire.' And he adds a note for the benefit of Alexander: 'Such ease and safety in our habitations, which when our death parts us from them, we yet leave the fruits of our labours to our children.'

From houses the transition is natural to cities and commerce, and he anticipates Adam Smith in his analysis of the advantages of a money economy over barter: 'Money will turn one thing into many, and many into one. . . so a countryman selling an ox for five pounds, buys with the same money sometimes thirty several things, when no man could tell how to cut his ox into so many several pieces.' Not only is England the equal of any other country in 'all mechanical arts', but 'we also have the liberal sciences so learnedly taught in our universities that we can hardly endure to have any other nation of the world to be allowed to compare with ours; yea, and perhaps have more learned men at this day in every shire than the whole kingdom could have yielded in former ages.' Finally, Richard speaks for the untitled aristocracy, the gentry, for whom the established hierarchy was ordained by God. 'We have our people placed in several ranks, according to their birth, estate and qualities, and each made thereby more helpful unto the others. So do the meaner sort by their labour maintain the greater in plenty; and the greater, richer and wiser take care to maintain the meaner in peace, virtue and justice. Then if any, never so great, presume to oppress and abuse us, we have our King's High Courts of Justice ready to punish such offences, and if those neglect their duty we have our King and Parliaments to correct anything that is amiss.' 'I may boldly say,' he concludes, 'no nation under the cope of heaven ever took so sweet and so large a draught of the unspeakable favour of our most gracious God as we have done, and daily do.'

Yet Richard was not altogether easy. Perhaps the King and his Parliament were not working quite in that so desirable harmony, 'these things at this day not so duly performed as they ought to be'. Again, 'Ever since Abraham's time, silver and gold have been most esteemed as the most precious metals,' but now they are too often 'abused to all kind of wickedness; to oppression, gluttony, drunkenness, bribery, lust, murder and treason.' And he adds a cautionary, and characteristic, story.

'How greedy are we of these transitory earthly shadows by which we labour so extremely in vain to please ourselves; for all this world is not able to satisfy any one man's desire, as methought I saw plainly by the conference I had with one who, having twenty pounds a year to live on, told me, if he could bring that to be thirty he would desire no more. When I asked whether if it were in his choice to have thirty or forty, which he would ask, he answered, thirty would serve his turn very well. When I told him he should be advised what he did, for if he had forty he might use but thirty if he had none occasion, but if he did ask but thirty he could never after make it forty, he confessed by and by he would ask forty. From forty he came to fifty, to an hundred, and then, because he had never been used to so much, he began to fear robbing, but when I told him how he might save himself from that, he said he would have one hundred. So we went within one quarter of an hour from the thirty pounds by the year to three hundred thousand. Yet I think that great sum would no more have satisfied his desire than his twenty pounds by the year did.' And he adds significantly: 'For great princes, which have much more, do not all employ it so well, and as long as more may be had, it never seems enough.' And finally, a delightful touch: 'During the little time the greatest and most voluptuous men enjoy their pleasures, I doubt much whether they can so soundly embrace their choicest delights as a poor boy doth his play with his top and his scourge.' Yet Richard himself was doing well enough at this time, for towards the end of his book he thanks God for having 'increased my living by almost doubling it within one year.'

God, of course, is not responsible for the failures and corruption of the age, for it must be remembered that 'as God hath made our natural bodies to have sudden and great alterations by sickness and other accidents, so hath he left bodies politic subject to the like.' The fault lies partly in man's frailty, ignorance and fallibility. 'All the natural knowledge we have here comes by our five senses, and every one of these is apt to be deceived: the eye by jugglers, the ears by echoes, the taste by agues, the feeling by misplacing the fingers, and the scent by the likeness of the savour of one thing to another.' Tell the wisest Indian who lives on the equator that in this country the cold turns rivers into so hard a stone that carriages can be driven over them, and he will only laugh at you. Tell an Irish peasant that it never rains in Egypt, and he will not believe you. Tell a countryman that on the coast the sea rises and falls, and he will reply that 'he has seen many waters go downward, but never saw any go upward, and that we may as finely persuade him the sky will come down that we may catch larks.' 'If we then with all our wit are still so unable to find the truth of these plain things that are every day before our eyes, yea and are so ignorant in ourselves that if we were enabled to make our children's bodies according to our own devising, what strange monsters would our arrogant ignorance produce? Methinks, then, the only sure course is wholly to trust God and distrust ourselves.'

Ultimately, of course, the fault lies with the Devil, for

Richard a character every bit as real as God. 'As our most gracious God made all things at the beginning very good, so hath the Devil by the sin of man made all good things to be most wickedly perverted to all manner of evil.' He has even perverted the use of the mariner's compass and the wonderful art of navigation, which God himself taught Noah, for now they are abused by the stronger to rob the weaker, and by princes, whose ships transport their armies to conquer distant countries. Then, 'when at the prayer of Joshua, God made the sun to stand still, that his servants might have thereby the longer light to be avenged of their enemies, and himself the greater glory, because the Devil saw it to be a miracle so manifest to all the world that the denying thereof was like to avail little, he raised a tale among the heathen that Jupiter (whom they worshipped as the supreme of their multitude of false gods) was in love with Alcmena, and how to satisfy his lust with her he doubled the length of the night, and then begat Hercules whom he made to be a famous conqueror, that by that fore-received fable he might oppose the truth of the only begotten Son of God, who opened the Kingdom of Heaven to all believers, whither He, in the sight of many witnesses, visibly ascended, as the Devil (falsely) would have had the heathen believe Hercules to have done.' No wonder Richard thought that the most miserable of men are those who try to outwit and master the Devil, who leads them on until they find themselves 'tied with huge and horrible chains to the pit of Hell.' This is the theme to which he constantly returns, and he gives a dozen well-attested stories to warn his children of this fearful danger.

There was the dreadful example of his uncle William Bligh, who died so miserably after becoming involved with the conjurer Frobisher. 'So have I heard of one Frobisher, who not long since was admitted to show some of his tricks before our late King James, and gave the King such reason as he conceived them to be done only by legerdemain; but I think he showed him not so much as he did to others, for sometime these men cannot do the same tricks before one which they do before others, because they are restrained by the power of God, and at other times because their good master will not suffer them to be too bold, for fear lest his helping hand, being espied in the play, might make the spectators look better to themselves than he would have them. Yet this man played strange tricks in divers of my friends' sight, as themselves (who were men of good understanding) confessed they were even amazed and afraid to see, especially before mine uncle Bligh of Botathan, who was a gentleman of good rank and fashion, and held by the best of our county to be a man of good discretion and no way apt to believe in toys.

'He himself told me, how being lodged in an inward room in London, this Frobisher came into the outer one to practise his skill, where seeing others look on, himself drew the nigher to do the like. There he saw him cast a ring fast on a garter which another stretched out, holding both ends fast in his hands, and when he had strangely got it on, would presently as strangely take it off again, whilst one still held fast both ends of the garter. Some said he had a secret spring in his ring by which he did it, and demanded whether he could do the same with another ring. When he answered, "With any," mine uncle plucks off his ring which he wore on his finger, and Frobisher flung it on and took it off as he had done before, and within a while hurls the ring (to their seeming) right against the window, when they heard such a crash as glass makes when it is broken. Then says he to my uncle, "What is become of your ring?" He said, "You have thrown it out into the street." "No," says he, "it is in the tip of the finger of the gentleman's glove that came last into the room." As soon as the gentleman heard him say so, he answered, "I came but even now out of my study, and know not whether I have left my gloves behind me. I will therefore look in my pocket and see." Then he took out his gloves, and in them found the ring which they thought Frobisher had thrown out at the window.'

Apparently Frobisher had more than one accomplice, for next entered 'one in black', who summoned him gravely into a private room. The inquisitive Bligh could not help asking what his business was, and Frobisher told him that his visitor was a merchant whose ship and cargo had been reported lost, but that, in return for £20, he had guaranteed its safety, and the ship had just returned. Uncle Bligh, much impressed, then began to unburden himself: 'I have had strange fortune in my days of late—' but Frobisher anticipated him: ' "You have two which come to your house under colour of seeking alms, which do you no good nor wish you any," and he described two persons which resorted to his house as plainly as if he had seen them before him, and withal told him: "If you will be ruled by me, if ever hereafter they come on your ground with a purpose to hurt you, they shall never have the power to go out again," then told him what he would have him do.' The horrified Richard implored his uncle to do no such thing, 'for, if you had done what he told you, and thereby those persons had been bewitched to death, and had accused you for being his instrument therein, how could you have acquitted yourself?'

'These things mine uncle told me himself, and I have heard by others that he told him such a secret marks of his wife's body as, though they had been married sixteen or seventeen years, and the other had never seen her, at his return he found them to be such as he told him. And after he once talked with this man his life grew full of trouble, and he died with grief at last.' The only consolation was that Frobisher, 'as I believe, died a beggar, because men of his trade very seldom do other.'

The Devil does not work only through men, but sometimes uses women as his agents, and 'pretty little petty devils which they call fairies'. There was, for example, Joan Lobb, much resorted to by people from all over Cornwall and Devon. Once when Richard's cousin went to have a sore leg cured, Joan asked her: ' "Mistress, why are you so sad?" She answered, "I am not sad," but the other replied, "I wis but you be, and I know the cause, for you are in love with one whose name is Thomas. But set your heart at rest, you shall have him, and though he be a younger brother now, he shall sit in his father's seat." Which was true, and came so to pass. And as they were ready to go away, the old woman looked very earnestly upon a couple of my aunt's men who came with my cousin for company, which when they perceived, one of them said unto her in jest, "Mother Lobb, why do you look so on us? I hope you can say no other of us but that we are honest men." "That's true indeed," says she, "for you have each of you a bastard," saying to the one, "Yours is a boy," and to the other, "and yours is a maid," which they then thought could not have been known, they kept it so secret.' Poor Joan Lobb; she professed to do nothing but good, and would help none but good people, but the Devil will 'counterfeit an angel of light that he may draw man into mischief.'

The woman whose eyes goggled in her head when she seized Richard's hand to tell his fortune so many years ago told him that her skill was a gift given her by the stars, but she knew that Joan Lobb did what she did by the fairies. 'When I replied, "That was the Devil who made a fair show to Eve when he persuaded her to taste of the forbidden fruit, but thereby brought death into the world, and makes us all smart for it at this day," she added, "Ay, and he made her believe she should lose that she went withal if she did not eat thereof." Which, though the Scripture manifest to be a gross lie, yet I could not but wonder what an excellent excuse the Devil had newly devised to abuse an ignorant woman with, by persuading her that it was Eve's longing to save her child that made her eat thereof. After meeting this woman again in another place, one who knew her better than myself told me she had been Raw Clyes's servant, who was the man who conjured for my neighbour Chark's sail, by which I knew better than before how narrowly I escaped when I first saw her.

'And what extreme peril did those two gentlemen of our country (as I was told by a brother-in-law of theirs and a kinsman of mine) put themselves into with one Baker, who was notoriously known for a witch. When one of them told him, "I pray thee, Baker, if thou hast such extraordinary powers, show us a devil," he undertook to do it, and takes a set of counters out of his pocket and falls to work with them, as men use to do when they cast an account, but made so foul a reckoning that the fair day became stormy, and it began to thunder and lighten so directly in those gentlemen's faces that the one for fear ran out of the chamber, and the other desired him for God's sake to give over, for he could abide it no longer.

'Another, almost as strange as this, was I told by a gentleman of this country, who is well known to the King, and I repeat it from his own mouth: how once in the Strand, when he and a friend were leaning on the rails which then stood before Somerset House, one Captain Bubb, who was acquainted with one of them saluting him asked, "Whither dine you today?" The other answered, "I may dine any where, for I am bid no where." Thereupon says the other gentleman, "If it please you both to go with me to the Devil (for so they then called a tavern in Fleet Street) I will bestow a dinner upon you," which they kindly accepted. And when they were there private together, says he which was acquainted with Bubb, "You were wont to have some tricks of merriment for your friends. I pray you show this gentleman some sport." "I will," says he, and withal takes a ball of strange dice (which had crowns and characters upon them) out of his pocket and flirts them, which when he had done three or four times, he who was acquainted with him asked, "What mean you by this?" The other answered, "What will you say now if I will tell you of a thing you did sixteen years ago, which yourself will acknowledge no man could tell me of?" He replies, "That would be very strange." "Then," says he, "remember what passed between you and your hostess in the back side in Cork in Ireland so long since." '

Bubb was later punished as a cheater, but this, of course, in no way disproved that he had worked through a wicked spirit that had since betrayed him, 'for the Devil ever concludes with mischief to those who employ him.' Dr Burcot, it will be remembered, died a beggar, so did Frobisher, and then there was the wizard who could see the future in a shoulder of mutton, a joint that seems to have had a peculiar fascination for Richard. One morning, when on service in Ireland, this man, after gazing earnestly at his bone, prophesied that the day's expedition would end in disaster, and that some of their party would fail to return. He was right: they fell into an ambush, 'and among the slain there lay the wizard to prove the prediction true.'

This story reminded Richard of a similar one of 'these late and lamentable wars the Turks have made against the Christians.' These Barbary pirates also had their wizards, one of whom told the crew of a ship that they would be defeated. They therefore watched continually two days and two nights, until, overcome by weariness, they fell asleep. Then a few Christians whom they had taken prisoner 'fell upon them and cut all their throats like so many calves, before they had the time to awake and know who did it.' These Turks, Richard adds, 'have paper pictures in books of white men, whom they call Christians, and of black men for themselves, which divers Christians have affirmed to have seen to rise up and fall down upon one another as the success should follow.'

These unlawful dealings with the Devil were practised nearer home than the high seas. Only four miles from Antony House, at Wotton, the high-seated house of Richard's cousins, Peter and Sir William Courtenay, there was a carpenter who could foretell the exact day of birth of an illegitimate child the day after it had been secretly begotten. (Bastards were another of Richard's obsessions.) He terrified the maids of the house, and one day, to test his powers, they stuck a pin up to its head in one of the trees in the orchard, and challenged him to find it. ' "Pooh," he said, "that is a small matter," ' and went as readily to the place and fetched out the pin as they themselves could have done. And he would often say, if his skill were known he should be esteemed more than he was, for he said there was nothing done in the secretest chamber of the greatest prince in the world, but if he listed he would know it presently. And by this we may perceive how far plain and ignorant men can by the help of a wicked spirit outgo the wisest and most learned in the best arts which human understanding can naturally reach unto.'

Most terrifying of all, perhaps, was 'the most miserable end one John Cundy (who dwelt by Holsworthy) made within these few years. He, missing a horse and some of his sheep, was not content to seek for news of them by the ordinary and long way of inquiry, but to recover them (as he thought) more surely and quickly, he went to a conjurer to have him tell where they were, who agreed with him that when he had found them according to his direction, he should give so much as they agreed on for telling him where they were. Then, going to the place and finding them, he brought them home. After, the conjurer comes to have his wages, of which Cundy would pay but the one half, and though the other told him if he paid not the whole it should be the worse for him, yet he still refused to pay him any more.

'Within a while after, when this Cundy lay on his bed one morning, there came a tall man in black and went in unto him, and asked him if he would arise and meet him at the place appointed, and said, if he did not, it should be the worse for him; and so went out again, and left behind him a strong savour of brimstone. Whereon, there being some matches then laid in the oven to dry, his maid servant went to see whether any of them had taken fire, but though the smell continued they could find no cause thereof.

'After, arises Cundy and puts on his old clothes, and the maid who heard speak of the meeting supposed it had been to some market about his business, therefore asked him why he would not put on his best clothes. He answered, they were good enough, and calls a boy, his nephew, to go with him, and so they went together to the field where the sheep were. And when he was come to the middle of the field, he bade the boy go home again. The boy was scarce gone out of the field when he saw a terrible flash of lightning and heard a great clap of thunder, and looking about saw his uncle killed, the ground torn under him, his body and clothes burning, for the fire consumed one of his legs to the knee, burned off one of his ears and a piece of his nose, and made all the silver in his purse look like brass. And I was told this by one who came to see him where he lay, ere the fire was gone out of his clothes, and he said this thunder and lightning came suddenly, the weather being fair before and presently after, yet the trees thereby were blasted as if it had been done with fire.'

Richard concludes this section of his book, enchantingly called 'The Imperial Conjurer and the Carpenter', on a note of self-congratulation: that he and his family are beyond the reach of the Devil, unlike those who think they can command him by incantations, making circles and other damnable devices, and those who vainly and wickedly imagine they can make use of witches, wizards and conjurers for their own ends. 'And I have the more willingly written these strange and true stories, that it may plainly appear that the wicked, blasphemous, drunken, ambitious and covetous gallants of our age might easily see the notorious acts of the Devil so manifestly proved by the testimony of so many credible witnesses. Yet it is no marvel if they who refuse to believe the word of God will not believe any man, because their understandings are blinded by their lusts.'

The goodness and power of God are everywhere to be seen by those who are not thus blinded. Consider the wonder of writing: 'for by a little ink and paper one man can convey his thoughts to another, though as far asunder as the Antipodes; by which all the arts have been preserved and are daily increased; by which we can speak a thousand years after we are dead and rotten; by which God himself hath revealed unto us His wonderful works and Holy Word.' As for printing, 'the perfection it hath now found shows plainly that it was God's and not man's work, for the good of his chosen children.'

Even 'the fishes of the sea daily declare the wonderful wisdom and goodness of God,' for by ordaining the seventh day for His service, he prevents our over-fishing the waters. And then, consider the confusion if whales were to breed on the same scale as herrings and pilchards. But thanks to God, the bigger the fish the fewer its offspring, so that all the multitudinous smaller fry are not devoured, but are lured to the shore by the warmth of shallow water, to the great profit and advantage of man.

Not only are God's visible works proof of His invisible power, they are also proof of the truth of the Scriptures. In Cornwall, for example, there is clear evidence of the Flood, which, as it advanced from the country of Noah, gradually submerging the mountains of Europe, washed down the loose tin from the hills, leaving streams of ore running from east to west, as well as huge trees which, overturned by the great waters, tinners now find buried deep in the earth.

'Then, as I have heard, the fruits which grow on the trees near adjoining the Dead Sea where Sodom and Gomorrah stood, bear apples which in ordinary shape resemble others, but within contain nothing but a kind of ashes, for a perpetual memorial of their fearful punishment by fire from heaven. And we know the last end of the world, as God hath revealed in His Word, shall be by fire, of the near approaching of which uncertain, yet most assured time, the tokens fulfil apace. And as God, when He rained water from Heaven and opened the fountains of the deep that both might join together to cover the earth, so hath He (even in my days) made many coal mines to be discovered in such places as were never thought to contain any such matter, thereby to warn us that in the very beginning He prepared for the very last ending of all, and hath given us use of those treasures of fire, and warning by them, how ready they are to execute His judgments when He shall command them to become fountains of fire for the burning of all.'

It was the early summer of 1630 when Richard began the last section of his book, 'An Exhortation out of mine own Affection to have everybody partake of my greatest Joy and Happiness.' He was now nearly fifty, and had written for almost two years, filling more than two hundred folio pages, and during this time he had buried his mother in Antony church next to his father, beside whom he had reserved a space for himself. He felt that his work had not been wasted, neither had it gone unappreciated in the right quarters, for not only had his income been doubled while he was writing, but his decaying sight had been restored by the use of spectacles, so that he might complete his labours.

The great test, however, was yet to come, his dearest wish still to be fulfilled: 'O that my blessed Saviour would now give me that holy and powerful Spirit that by the mouth of St Peter gained three thousand souls unto the Church in one day, and so guide my pen that thereby I might make the hearts of multitudes of men so sensible of their sins that they might prick them with a fervent desire to be saved from this froward generation we now live in! For surely the harvest is great, and the labourers are few. And how happy are we whom Thou hast elected and selected from the innumerable multitude (which pass from the short death of the body to the everlasting death of the soul, where the worm of conscience for sin never dieth, nor the fire of torment ever goeth out), who shall suddenly be taken up into the most glorious Kingdom of Heaven, and there have an everlasting new life!'

Knowing that the flames of Hell were for others, not for him, it is no wonder that Richard finished his book with thanks to God for having taken such a personal interest in his welfare. 'O blessed Saviour! what thanks can I render unto Thee for giving me so long a time and such grace to repent, and such assurance to preserve me against all future dangers by Thy never failing power, and teaching me Thy Holy Spirit to cast all my care on Thee both for this life and that to come, and assuring me by Thy Holy Word that none shall ever be able to withdraw Thy love from me, nor to keep me from enjoying everlasting happiness in Thine own presence, in the due time Thou hast appointed for me.'

Soon after he had written the last word of his book, 'me', his son Alexander came of age, and it was probably to celebrate the event that his father commissioned the painting of his portrait. It still hangs in Antony House, a splendid full-length picture of the young man, in scarlet breeches and yellow jerkin, the head rather small for the body, and in the delicate features we seem to detect those of his mother, Bridget, who had died before he was two. Richard had written his book as another twenty-first birthday present, a guide for the next Carew of Antony, but it is clear that he meant to publish, for he tells us that he wrote for his Christian brethren as well as, even more than, for his children, 'for the natural obligation is not so great as the spiritual,' and only by publishing could he reach those multitudes whom he hoped to save from everlasting damnation.

He was disappointed, however, for even in that puritanical age publishers were daunted by the endless paragraphs of pious exhortation and pages of lofty exclamation, and the book remained a manuscript in Richard's study, where Alexander dutifully read it. No doubt John, who was only eight in 1630, was soon introduced to it.

One wonders what they made of it, and what they thought of their father. Certainly his sons could not have seen him as we do, objectively, more than three centuries later, in a far more sceptical age. Did Alexander yawn as he quickly turned over the pages of pious exaltation and apostrophe—'O! in how great uncertainty doth every man enjoy this poor life!' 'O blessed Saviour! what a wonder, more beyond all wonders. . .' 'O God! how wondrous are thy works!'? And did he smile when he read the Socratic arguings with which his father invariably discomfited his opponents? Unfortunately, it seems improbable that he did. We can see Richard as an obstinate, self-opinionated, complacent and pompous busybody, over-occupied with his spiritual and physical welfare; the most credulous of men, avidly absorbing anecdotes that made his flesh creep and tingle with pleasurable horror at the thought of other's peril and his own security; a potential persecutor of poor wretches like Joan Lobb, and all those whom he suspected of being in league with the Devil.

Yet this unlovely trait he shared with many of his devout contemporaries, and he had virtues that far outweighed his frailities. Although he would have rid the country of calkers, witches and wizards, there was no cruelty in his nature, but a vein of compassion that was exceptional in his age, and must have distinguished him from most of his fellow men. 'The power which God hath given us over all his creatures, how imperiously do we always use in taking away the sheep's clothes to clothe ourselves, their milk from their young to feed ourselves, nay their lives to maintain our own, though we cannot complain of any offence they have done, or that we fear they would ever do unto us. Nay, do not the greatest persons make it their principal pleasure to pursue the innocent creatures with hawking and hunting for their sport, unto death, and follow it so hard as if there was nothing else for them to do in he world? Yet the poorest worm is our fellow creature.' Despite his egocentricity, he was not a selfish man, but desperately anxious to do his duty by his fellows, to relieve suffering in this world, and by precept and example to avert it in the next. 'To do good,' is his constant refrain: 'the better to enable myself to do good,' 'that I might be doing more good.' He was indeed a good man, innocent in an uninnocent age, loyal, and conscientious in his pursuit of virtue, as in all things, attractively simple, apart from the tortured complexities of his religious fanaticism.

A grateful and dutiful son, an affectionate husband, a well-meaning and kindly father, he was devoted to his family, though, over-solicitous in his care and probably clumsy and ponderous in action, he must frequently have encumbered them with his help. Then, there is an intrusive and redeeming vein of humility in his self-conceit; acknowledging that he cannot approach his father in wisdom, he pledges himself to 'follow him as hard as I can in that he most esteemed, and for which he most esteemed me, true honesty.' An honest enthusiast and benevolent eccentric, he took himself too seriously, and must have been taken by others as something of a joke. But not by his children, by Alexander and John, who seem to have seen him as one of the Old Testament figures he so much admired and no doubt assumed; far from a figure of fun.

8

The Fateful Thirties

So Richard, Alexander and John entered the fateful decade of the 'thirties. Outwardly it was a peaceful period, for the King was determined to call no more Parliaments to quarrel with him, and without his Commons to vote supplies he could not afford the luxury of foreign adventure. Yet below the surface the fire of rebellion was beginning to smoulder.

To supplement the taxes on foreign trade, which he claimed as his right, Charles extracted money from the people, particularly the gentry, by reviving obsolete feudal dues, such as fines for failure to receive knighthood, and for infringement of the Norman forest laws. Then came an annual demand for ship money, a tax that the Tudors had occasionally levied in time of need for the maintenance of the navy. In these ways, not absolutely illegal, like forced loans, Charles was able to maintain and strengthen his despotism.

At the same time, his devoted servant Thomas Wentworth, later Earl of Strafford, was reducing Ireland to order and organizing an army for his master, while at home the new Archbishop of Canterbury, William Laud, was organizing the Church in his support, for he and his High Church party were fervent believers in the Divine Right of Kings. Puritans, a growing power, were forbidden to preach and had no chance of promotion, offices in the Church were filled with sound High Churchmen, the Prayer Book ritual was enforced, the Communion table was moved to the east end to serve as an altar, and those who met secretly to worship in their own simple way were arrested and imprisoned. As a result, thousands of Puritans followed the Pilgrim Fathers who had sailed from Plymouth in 1620—Richard must have seen them go—and settled in a New England in a New World.

Old England was fast becoming a despotism. Richard's neighbour, Sir John Eliot, died in the Tower in 1632, John Lilburne suffered for protesting against this arbitrary form of government, and John Hampden for refusing to pay ship money, but there was no organized form of revolt. In August 1636 Charles and his courtiers, many of whom had adopted the now fashionable Catholic creed, celebrated their triumph at Oxford with the High Churchmen, and Laud, Chancellor of the University, entertained them with a play satirizing the Puritans.

Meanwhile, during this first half of Charles I's personal government, Alexander Carew had married, to the confusion of Carew relationships, his stepmother's younger sister, Jane Rolle, and their first son, John, had been born. Then, in the spring of 1637, Richard had an accident, his description of which reads like the opening of a Defoe romance.

'The third day of this month of April in the year of our Lord 1637, seeking to get over a hedge that I might give directions to my workmen who were making a pool for me in the ditch on the other side, the weather being fair and the sun shining bright, and doubting lest a snake might lie in that warm place, as I looked carefully where I put my hands to take hold, my right foot slipped, and the weight of my body fell to bear on the innermost joint of my great toe, which put me to some pain, though yet but little. Therefore I thought it was only a small strain which would quickly wear away of itself, and so sate down by my workmen, and continued with them more than two hours ere feeling a little soreness, but not so much as deserved to be called by the name of pain. When I arose from thence, by favouring my hurt foot a little in my going, I returned to mine house where, when I had stayed but a while, I found my shoe too strait for my foot, therefore I put them off and put on my pantables [slippers], but they likewise, though it was supper time when I put them on, grew too strait for me before I went to bed.

'When I was abed I hoped that the rest of that place would ere the morning have cured me, but when I arose, thinking to have put on my clothes, I found my grief so much increased that I was forced to return to my bed again. There I found the swelling of my toe and foot became so great that I could not suffer my stockings upon my feet, though they were very large for me, therefore I was forced to take a larger stocking and slit him to give more room to my swelling flesh, and to endeavour to allay the pain by applying elder leaves, not only upon the place grieved, but a good way everywhere beyond it. So finding a little ease, having occasion to go to my study, though I succoured my foot as much as I could, both by myself and by the help of others, at my return my pain was so much increased that I had much to do to recover but a little sleeping time all that night.'

Thus, driven from his slippers to his bed, he reluctantly sent for a bonesetter, who found that the inner bone of his foot was 'cloven', and Richard, reproving himself for the neglect of his customary caution, resigned himself to a period of enforced idleness in bed. Not altogether idleness, however, for, reluctant to waste his precious time, he resolved, 'being unable to stir, to employ my mind in thanksgiving to God, for the manifold blessings He hath given me in the course of my life, for the recovery of such hurts and sicknesses as it hath pleased Him to visit me withal.' Then more cryptically, 'and to acknowledge the errors I have committed in the beginning of my life, which I have found in continuance of time with much abatement of my natural strength, so weakened now by accidents and age.' He was nearly fifty-seven, an old man in those days. But even in bed he could still do good, and calling for pen, ink and paper, he began to write an account of the remedies that he had found most efficacious for his own and others' maladies.

Of course he was his own physician in his latest misadventure, and we must imagine him sitting up in bed, his feet warmed by a hot stone wrapped in woollen cloths, and by his side a great pan of cold water into which he would thrust his hands and arms, often washing his face and back, and rinsing his mouth, but being very careful not to swallow any. For though his feet were cold, the rest of his body was hot, a condition that could not have been helped by the warm drink that he still insisted on.

And so he began to write: first on the merits of his greatest pride, his warming-stone. Applied to the bottom of the belly, it was a cure for the colic, as he knew from experience, and applied to the hinder parts, it eased those suffering from loose bellies and fluxes. It was excellent for rheums in the head, as well as for ruptures, as he and his father had found, and, as a weak old man, 'alive at this day', could testify. 'And,' he added, feeling the comfortable warmth of the stone at his feet, 'myself and many others have very often received much good by warming our feet therewith, both out of and in our beds. And that kind of baking-stone is best which will receive heat soonest and hold it longest, whereof we have one here in our country called a Polyphant stone, because it is digged out of the ground of a manor called by that name, which being well covered in my bed, hath kept a sensible heat for above nine hours.'

Then he turned to the defence of his warm diet. 'When they allege against me that it is a bad belly that cannot warm his own drink, I answer, "Whosoever would deny me warm drink should by the same reason never eat hot pottage." I add further what Sir William Strode told me, how his lady going once to visit a young woman of an hundred and ten years age, when she asked her what diet she had used to live so long, she answered, "Truly, madam, for these fifty years, winter nor summer, I have neither eaten nor drank any cold thing." Now I desire not to exceed her age.'

The advice of Parson Atwell, who had died just short of his century, had been, 'Keep full,' but Richard's was, 'Keep warm,' and when necessary, 'Keep empty'—and avoid salt, 'for salt breeds the stone exceedingly, and I much fear salt things do likewise breed and increase the gout. Therefore I hold it fit, when age denies men to live by the strength of their stomach, as lusty youths do with too much excess, that then they should seek to live by the strength of their understanding, so to choose and temper their diet, that though they cannot avoid the inseparable, troublesome companions of the stone, gout and palsy in treading upon their heels and toes before they are aware of it, yet they may never suffer them to ride upon their backs as long as they have power to stand up against them.' And he tells another characteristic story.

'Now, because my father and myself were subject unto the stone (for I cannot live long healthfully without breeding gravel in my water) for the cleansing thereof I use, as often as I find it needful, a large warm well-sugared posset with store of bread in it, to wash it clean away. And not long since, meeting with a gentleman of good rank and quality at a friend's house, being importunately intreated to sit at dinner with them, which I yielded unto upon condition not to be pressed to eat or drink anything, the other gentleman, who knew me not, seeing me abstain from touching any dish of so many delicate meats as that long table was fully furnished with, asked me why I kept such a precise diet, and said he thought I was much the worse for it; that himself having kept no diet, was both elder and stronger than myself with my too much daintiness, that he thanked God by that means he could feed heartily upon any dish on the table. I answered him I envied no man's prosperity in being more healthful and strong than myself, and yet I would fain know whether we did eat and drink to live, or live to eat and drink. If we did eat and drink to live, methought such a measure should be fittest as would best preserve and maintain health, but if we did live to eat and drink, then we might lay on load. I added further, that as good as his stomach was, he would be loth to be bound to eat all that was on the table. He said that were unreasonable. I replied it was as unreasonable for me to eat more than would do me good as it was for him.

'He then said he thanked God he was subject to no disease but one, which was enough to kill a horse, and that was the stone; then intreated me to guess how many he had avoided the first time that he found himself subject thereunto. After my excuses, he said that he had avoided seven score at once. His brother, at whose table we sat, said he avoided above two hundred at once, which though they were very little, yet were sensibly told. The other said his were far greater, as big as the smallest sort of pea.' After listening to this fraternal competition, Richard remarked, 'Perhaps, gentlemen, I can tell you somewhat may do you good,' and he had little difficulty in persuading them that their stones were bred of salt, and could be dissolved and washed away by plenty of warm liquor. As usual, his auditors were completely convinced of their error, and after a pause, 'the first gentleman said, "Sir, I believe you say true, for I think no man loves nor eats more salt and salt meats than myself." His brother said likewise, and after dinner both gave me very great thanks for what I had done.'

In this way Richard gained a considerable reputation, and people even came to consult him. With his warm diet he cured a young cousin 'overgrown with a consumption which he was fallen into with our hard study at Oxford'; and another young man in the same plight was sent to him by his friends, who despaired of his recovery, yet after a few weeks of the Antony *régime* he was completely restored. There were, however, complications; the young man took tobacco, and Richard insisted that he should stop smoking. He spoke severely: 'Where it doth one man good, it doth twenty, if not a hundred harm. It must be taken either for food or for physic, and if it be for food, it is such a strange one for man to live by as no other creature in the world doth the like, neither know I what substance can come from smoke but water and soot; if it be taken for physic, it is a very strange kind of physic which everyone that useth it hath such perpetual need of.' Yet he was less severe than King James on the same subject: 'A custome loathsome to the eye, hatefull to the nose, harmefull to the braine, dangerous to the lungs, and in the blacke stinking fume thereof, nearest resembling the horrible Stigian smoake of the pit that is bottomlesse.'

Richard admitted that there were occasions when a warming-stone and a hot drink were not entirely adequate: for example, your broken neck. 'When two servants of the house of Trerice, in which I was born, fell out and fought, the one thrust the other over a great and high bank, and in his fall pitched on his head, and so put his neck out of joint, and was not able to move.' His life was saved by the application of hot elderberry oil, though when Richard saw him three years later, he could not turn his neck, 'but was fain to turn his whole body withal.'

There were other simple remedies that he could recommend: veronica for the eyes—with it he had stayed his father's failing sight, and recovered that of one of his quarrymen; hart's-tongue for the yellow jaundice; boiled tar and boar's grease to ease a rupture; and he had a tip for avoiding the cramp, 'which is gartering the flesh before we go to bed.' But best of all were the therapeutic qualities of the elder. His own foot was swathed in elder leaves as he wrote, though it is true that it was beginning to look a little odd, being 'full of black spots and white between,' but for an ordinary bruise they were admirable. For example, when he rowed a lady and her husband across the river to Antony, 'when they came to enter the boat she fell upon the rocks and, being somewhat corpulent, bruised the cop of her knee so that the pain thereof made her shed tears and cry. I entreated her to have a little patience till we came to the shore, and then, knowing where elder trees grew fast by, fetched her a handful of the leaves and caused her to apply them to it, by which she was soon eased and fully cured.' Then, they had blessedly relieved the torturing pain of his corns, which had reduced his walk to a hobble. Unfortunately the elder is deciduous, but the evergreen ivy was an excellent substitute, and by basting its leaves inside his stockings, and changing them every day or two, he had at length quite rid himself of the pain.

Poor Richard, he needed all his courage to write his book with such conviction. He was pestered with the well-meant advice of friends, and a physician, hearing of his sickness, prophesied that it would eventually turn into a dropsy. Then, despite the elder leaves, his foot looked more and more unwholesome; he began to fear gangrene, that it would have to be cut off, fears that of course he kept to himself. Finally, and perhaps the shrewdest blow of all, his warm diet failed him, making him so feverish that he was reduced to drinking the cold milk that he so much detested, with the result that, as he foresaw, he was soon 'bound extremely, and grieved with the piles.'

At last, however, his foot began to improve, and he recovered sufficiently to ride half a dozen miles to 'an extraordinary meeting of our kindred and friends', perhaps a party to celebrate another addition to Alexander's rapidly growing family. 'But the meal continuing much longer than common ones use to do, this continual sitting made me, ere I was aware, to drink more than my weak stomach was able to turn into fit nourishment, and so made me sensible of my unwary excess that within two days after my return my sore leg brake out with a fiery heat all over, and a kind of scalding water which ran through both the leaves and the linen, which I applied thereunto to ease it, in such sort as one of mine own children, whom God hath been pleased to bless with the curing of many persons, out of her chartiable affection to do them as much good as she could, told me that she thought the medicine was too strong and drawing for my grief; but I answered her, the fault was in myself and not in the medicine, and that I must amend mine excess by abstinence.'

As ever, he was right, and all was well: 'Blessed be God, I have now altogether recovered my infirmities, and have the use of my leg and body as sound as, according to the weakness of my age and constitution, I could well expect; neither was this abstinence anything near so painful unto me as my purge was which I took when I was in France in the strength of my youth.'

He composed his peroration with particular care: 'Now, if it please God to make me so happy as to have these, my slender reasons, struck out of the poor steel of my weak nature by the force of the hard flint of necessity, that any spark thereof lighting upon the delicate tinder of any physician excellent for knowledge and practice in that deep and secret art of nature, fairly to correct my unwilling mistakes herein. . . I shall be wondrous glad to have given but a poor occasion to have such an excellent work come to light for the glory of God and good of mankind.' Evidently he hoped to publish, but again he was disappointed, and he gave his manuscript to Mrs Buller.

It must have been midsummer before he was again hobbling about the grounds of Antony House, his stockings stuffed with elder leaves and ivy. He would then hear what had happened to three Puritans who had dared to write against the bishops and the lax observance of Sunday. Arraigned before the Star Chamber, they were sentenced to the pillory, branding, loss of their ears, and imprisonment for life. One of them, Prynne, a lawyer, had already lost his ears for attacking stage plays, and when the executioner sawed off the stumps in Palace Yard, a great cry rose from the asembled crowd. It was the first public protest against the tyranny of Charles I.

A month later, July 1637, the revolution began. With almost incredible folly Charles tried to impose Laud's High Church system on the Presbyterian Scots, ordering the adoption of a Prayer Book similar to that of the English Church, in place of Knox's Book of Common Order. Everywhere there were riots, resistance was organized, and almost every Scot south of the Catholic Highlands signed a National Covenant and declaration of faith. In November 1638 a General Assembly met in Glasgow and swept away all Charles's changes; episcopacy was abolished, and the Presbyterian system re-established.

There was no standing army in England, and to crush this rebellion Charles had to rely on the northern trainbands, peasants eager only to return to their fields, and officered by gentry who sympathized with the Scots. Such a force was quite incapable of meeting the disciplined and determined Scottish army, and Charles had to disband his militia and agree to a truce. Having gained time, he tried to raise an efficient army, but for this he needed money, and to get money he had to summon Parliament. The eleven years of personal government were over. But the 'Short Parliament' that met in April 1640 was opposed to the 'Bishops' War', and refused to grant supplies until their grievances were redressed and liberties secure. Charles had called it to support, not to question, his policy, and at the beginning of May he dissolved it. He thought that he could afford to do so, for Strafford had returned to help him, determined to impose on England a despotism as efficient as that by which he had subdued Ireland.

9

The Baronet

This, then, was the political situation in the early summer of 1640: the King and Strafford preparing to establish an even more thorough despotism—'Thorough' was Strafford's watchword—and to create an army that would crush the Scots and overawe the English, while the peoples of the two countries were drawing closer together in a common effort to resist tyranny. There were riots in many parts of the country; in London gangs of apprentices roamed the streets in search of Laud, and even in conservative Cornwall discontent was growing at the calling up of the militia and levying of ship money to finance a war on the distant Scottish border.

Richard tells us nothing about these things, but he had much to say about the fearful happenings in Antony church on Whit Sunday, 24 May 1640. He himself had been unable to attend Communion that morning 'by reason of sickness', but his eldest daughter Elizabeth, 'the widow Pearse', was there, and ran back with the exciting news. There were about two hundred in the congregation, and while Mr Bache was administering the Communion at the table—it is significant that there was a table, not a Laudian altar, at Antony—a lightning in the form of a fiery ball broke through one of the chancel windows; there was a hissing like that of a great shot, and then the ball exploded with a terrible report, leaving a loathsome smell of gunpowder and brimstone. It was deliciously like the miserable end of John Cundy (who dwelt by Holsworthy) save that nobody was fatally injured, in spite of other sheets of flame that entered by various windows, and the only casualties were one dog in the chancel, another by the belfry door, and a horse in the field outside. Moreover, Elizabeth assured her father, if he had himself been there, he would have had nothing to fear, for though the fiery ball broke through the window immediately behind where he would have been sitting, 'and strake Nicholas Skelton with such violence as if he had been stricken with two flat stones, the one on the one side and the other on the other side of his head,' it ran all round his seat before rushing up the chancel and killing the dog, which she heard 'only once to screech'. Then, although the communicants were thrown about by the explosion, and there was a confusion of groans and cries, there was no panic, and nobody left the church until the service was finished.

It was the most exciting thing that had ever happened at Antony; Richard forgot his sickness, and spent one of the happiest weeks of his life interviewing in his study those who had been afflicted. As it had been the 'third table' who were waiting for their wine when the explosion occurred, most of the testifiers belonged to the lower orders: John Gendle, Nicholas Wilcock, servants of Richard's, John Hodge, Ferdinando Reep and the rest.

'Mr Bache, the minister of our parish'—again it is significant that he was a 'minister', not one of your High Church priests or vicars—Mr Bache 'was stricken on the left side of the head and the outside of the left leg, in such sort as that he verily thought that the hair of his head had been burned off and his leg scalded,' and if he had not just then moved towards the Communion table with the cup he would inevitably have been killed.

'Dorothy Tubbe, kneeling at the receiving of the Communion, was smitten so with the lightning that it seemed to her that her knees and legs were stricken off from her body, wherewith she was astonished.

'Susanna Collin also received a grievous blow as if she had been struck with fire, and the under part of her body seemed as if it had been severed from the upper, and scalded the wrist of her right arm as broad as a piece of three pence, which continued raw and red a whole week after.' The witnesses were doing their best to please their eccentric old squire, and enjoying themselves as much as he was.

'Anthony Peeke was also stricken in all the lower part of his body, as if he had been made dead, and felt the water in his bladder boiling hot, and supposed he had been shot, and was set up upon the form where he was kneeling, himself not knowing how.

'William Sargent, also kneeling a little off from the chancel window, was stricken on the chine with so grievous a blow that it seemed his body was cut in two, and his water violently issued from him, and for a time lost his sight and senses; who for two or three years before, feeling pain in his chine, was hereby so cured as he felt no pain there since.'

It was a miracle. Not only would he himself have been unhurt, but Mr Bache had been miraculously saved, and William Sargent had actually been healed by the visitation. It was also a revelation, and Richard wrote a little pamphlet about it, which he called 'The Voice of the Lord in the Temple'. 'I, Richard Carew of Antony (who as carefully as possibly I could) received all these informations from the mouths of each party, do no less humbly and thankfully acknowledge the wonderful favour of Almighty God than if I had been presently delivered from it, for I verily believe I should have been as safely preserved if I had been there, as I was at home. And I humbly praise God in the behalf of all the congregation, and most heartily desire that every one of us who have received this great deliverance (the like whereof was never heard from any of our forefathers) may never forget it, and so recommend it to our posterity from generation to generation, that it may continue unto the end of the world unto the honour and glory of God.'

Stimulated by these momentous events and the writing of his account, Richard turned again to literary composition, and in October sent his manuscript to the London publisher, John Bartlet. It was called *Excellent Helps by a Warming-Stone*. His essay begins with a description of his invention, and an account of the occasions on which he himself had found comfort in a stone: when dangerously oppressed with often and much vomiting, when grievously pained and tortured with the colic, when his feet had been cold, when his hands had been frozen as he sat in that icy chancel of Antony church over the bones of his ancestors, once when he hurt his foot climbing over a hedge, and now, when the natural heat of his own person had decayed, and cold become a chronic malady. And he remembered how he had comforted Bridget after the birth of Elizabeth, so many years ago now, by putting a warmed stone at the lower end of her bed, by which means she came to sweat as kindly as possibly could be. The rest is a series of testified cases: of how Richard Rumble was eased of a rupture, Theophila Deeble of Antony cured of a pain in the head, Philip Collin, also of Antony, of weakness and coldness (perhaps Philip was the husband of Susanna Collin who had been so grievously struck by the fiery ball that she fell sidewise where she kneeled). It was invaluable for scholars in studies, he added, thinking of his own literary labours, and there really was no complaint, from the cradle to the grave, that would not be cured or eased by the warming stone. 'And I hope,' he concluded, 'many millions hereafter may be saved hereby, and with this advantage also, that abundance of fuel may be saved everywhere.'

He took this opportunity of sending to Bartlet a few of his earlier compositions, what he modestly called his 'toys'. on the teaching of languages: 'I send you also 2 or 3 little toys of mine owne conceit, how children may be more easily taught both Latin and English than is used by the common practice; which if upon the reading you conceive to be grounded upon sound reason, you may impart them to more learned and understanding men than myself, and if they can produce any good, I shall be very glad of it. If not, I pray return them to me again.' He describes his own youthful drudgery of learning Latin grammar for nine or ten years, and complains that he was taught no living European language, so that when he went to Poland, Sweden and France he was compelled to try to make himself understood in Latin. However, he taught himself

French by reading and conversation, and cites his father, who taught himself five languages, 'only by reading'. His conclusion is an enlightened one: the orthodox method is literally preposterous; grammar should be studied last, not first, and children not wearied with a subject that makes them dislike the language, but should have their interest aroused in the literature by reading and translation: 'Whereby they should in that wasted time of their youth gain the knowledge of many good authors which they could not have time to read, and which by their dullness in learning the rules of grammar, they are so tired with the difficulty thereof that they conceive an impossibility ever to attain it, and so quit it.' In this at least, Richard was centuries ahead of his age.

By the autumn of 1640, however, Bartlet had other things to think of, more important pamphlets to publish than essays on warming stones and Latin grammar. Events had moved quickly during the summer: members of the last Parliament had been thrown into prison, the bishops had issued a new set of High Church canons, and by means of a forced loan, ship money and the press gang, Strafford had raised an army of a sort. With this mutinous and largely Puritan rabble he moved north, but in August the Scots contemptuously brushed it aside, seized Newcastle as their headquarters, and occupied Northumberland and Durham. Not only had Charles to agree to their political and religious demands, but he had also to pay their expenses, £25,000 a month, before they would retire. There was nothing for it but to summon another Parliament, and on 3 November it met. A week later the Commons, led by Pym, accused Strafford of attempting to subvert the fundamental laws of the kingdom, arrested him and sent him to the Tower, where he was soon joined by the aged Laud.

In the Commons the Cornish contingent of forty-four—two for the county, and forty-two for the boroughs—formed almost a tenth of the total members. One of the members for the county was Sir Bevil Grenville, grandson of Sir Richard of the *Revenge*, and the best loved man in Cornwall. The imprisonment and death in the Tower of his great friend Eliot had made him for a time a leader of the opposition to the royal despotism, but the Scottish war restored his innate loyalty, and it was as a supporter of the King that he rode up to London to take his seat in Parliament.

The other county member was Alexander Carew, who had just celebrated his thirty-first birthday.

Two great issues faced the Long Parliament. One was political: the limitation of the royal authority and restoration of the liberties of the subject. The other was religious: to safeguard the Protestant Church and prevent 'innovations in religion', for there was a very real fear that the Laudian High Church was only the prelude and lever to the restoration of Roman Catholicism. Over the political issue Parliament was at first virtually unanimous, and passed a series of measures that reduced the crown to complete financial dependence on itself, and established the principles of a limited monarchy.

Then in March 1641 came the impeachment of Strafford in Westminster Hall. Before the House of Lords, his judges, Pym sought to prove that he had been guilty of treason against the State, but as treason was legally defined as 'levying war against the King', the Lords could not find him guilty. The more extreme members of the Commons thereupon demanded an Act of Attainder, a means that had sometimes been employed by the Tudors to rid themselves of a troublesome subject without trial. Eight of the Cornish members voted against the Bill, and during its final reading Grenville turned to Alexander Carew with: 'Pray, Sir, let it not be said that any member of our county should have a hand in this ominous business, and therefore pray give your vote against this Bill.' To which Alexander replied: 'If I were to be sure to be the next man that should suffer upon the same scaffold with the same axe, I would give my consent to the passing of it.' The Bill was passed, and the King compelled to sign the death warrant of his most loyal friend and supporter, and on 12 May he was executed.

A week before the execution of Strafford, a resolution had been submitted to the Commons: 'to defend the true Protestant religion, His Majesty's Royal Person, Honour and Estate, the

Power and Privilege of Parliament, and the lawful Rights and Liberties of the Subject.' Provided the King renounced Laud and his Anglican innovations, and recognized Parliament as a partner in the government of the country, the Commons would support him. Two in three of the Cornish members signed, among them Alexander. Parliament was beginning to divide.

In August the King went to Scotland, and while he was away the more extreme Puritans introduced a Root and Branch Bill 'for the utter abolition of archbishops, bishops, archdeacons, prebendaries and canons'. Francis Rous, Richard's old friend, and one of the members for Truro, led this attack on episcopacy, but there is no record of what part Alexander played in the debate. Those, however, who loved the Church of England and its Prayer Book, were alienated, like Edward Hyde, later Earl of Clarendon, and when Parliament adjourned in September it was almost equally divided.

Meanwhile, in remote Antony, Richard was still in the literary vein, and it was in this critical year of 1641 that he wrote to Samuel Hartlib, the educationist and agriculturist, asking him to tell Bartlet that, 'I am about to fitt a Booke which shall direct all men both how to make Fruit-trees grow in abundance of the same kind that the graffe was, without graffing; and also how to multiply all sorts of Timber Trees, and make them grow more speedily than the ordinary way, and to longer bodies of Timber, and likewise in such places as without help they can never naturally doe. . . And I dare boldly say that the Invention will appeare, upon Tryall, to bee the most proffitable for mankind in generall, which hath beene found out in things of this Nature, above these 2000 yeares.' Richard was ever an optimist; but the book was never published, perhaps never written, though the fact that he was contemplating such a work at this time suggests that he took little interest in the events that were leading up to civil war. On the other hand, he might have sought refuge and distraction from them in writing about his beloved fruit trees, and how, when he had married Bridget forty years before, he made his orchards his delight, calling his pear trees his hawks and apple trees his hounds.

Then, on 5 August he was created a baronet. The patent conferring the baronetcy is preserved at Antony House, an impressive square yard of parchment with a seal as big as a saucer, on one side Charles I enthroned, on the other on horseback enjoying the delights of the chase. The long Latin inscription has much to say about the pleasures and privileges of being a baronet, but nothing about the merits of Richard, or what he had done to deserve the honour. His recent dissertation on the Warming-Stone can scarcely have been an adequate reason for the award.

The order of the baronetcy had been instituted in 1611 by James I as 'a new Dignitie between Barons and Knights', his object being to raise money for the Crown—'that the Kinges wants might be much relieved out of the vanities and ambition of the gentrie'—the consideration being £1,000. James's lavish creation of knights and baronets had been an occasion for much contemporary satire, and for Charles I the sale of baronetcies was an obvious way of raising money legally. In 1641 blank patents were offered at a considerable discount, baronetcies could be snapped up for £400 or even £350 apiece, and there can be little doubt that Richard was one of those who took advantage of this sensational reduction of price.

It is true that during the Civil War Charles sometimes conferred the honour on ardent Royalists without expecting, or at least demanding, payment, but there is no reason to think that Richard was thus honoured before the war began. He was not above vanity, not even above worldly ambition, yet if he paid £400 (some £7,000 today) to the King, either his sympathies were with him, or he was acting quite irresponsibly and cynically. Irresponsibility and cynicism, however, were failings quite foreign to Richard's character. He was a Puritan, fanatically devout, but, although he must have disapproved of Laud's High Church, there is nothing in his writings to suggest that he would have urged the abolition of episcopacy, and ten years earlier—admittedly at the beginning of Charles's personal government—he had prayed that he and his family might 'express in all things we may an extraordinary love to our princes, who hold their crowns immediately by the Grace of God.' Alexander, who had just voted for the execution of Strafford, cannot have approved of his father's contribution to the King, nor can John, Alexander's half-brother, now nineteen and a student of the Inner Temple, and it may be that as the Houses of Parliament were beginning to divide, so was the House of Antony.

By the time Parliament reassembled, many of the members who had supported Pym in the previous session had modified their opinions or even changed their allegiance, and when Pym introduced the Grand Remonstrance, a declaration of no confidence in the King, it was carried by only eleven votes. Three days later, on 25 November, Charles returned from Scotland, and finding that the tide had turned in his favour he decided to take the offensive. On 4 January 1642, accompanied by a rout of 'cavaliers', he entered the House of Commons to arrest his leading opponents, Pym, Hampden, Hazlerigg, Holles and Strode, the last related by marriage to the Chudleighs, and therefore to the Carews. But the five members had been warned, and had fled to the protection of the London trainbands in the City. There were great demonstrations in their favour, and after the King's flight from Whitehall on 10 January they returned in triumph to Westminster. It was the final breach, and for the next eight months Royalists and Parliamentarians prepared for war. When it came, London and the south-east, the navy and ports were mainly for Parliament, while the more backward north and west on the whole supported the King.

Everywhere, however, loyalties were divided: a man might be Puritan yet Royalist, Anglican yet Parliamentarian, and in Cornwall, although most of the great families were for the King, some stood firm for Parliament. Among the leading Royalists were Sir Bevil Grenville, Sir Francis Godolphin and Sir John Arundell of Trerice, Richard's uncle; among the leading Parliamentarians were Lord Robartes of Lanhydrock,

Sir Richard Buller of Shillingham and Alexander Carew of Antony. It was the religious rather than the political issue that divided Cornwall, so that the Parliamentary party was strongest in the east, near Plymouth, where Puritanism was strongest, but most of the clergy were loyal to the Anglican Church, and carried their parishioners with them into the Royalist camp.

As there was no standing army, each side tried to gain control of the county militias, and at Lostwithiel in June, Grenville, Arundell and others issued commissions in the King's name. A month later Alexander was one of those sent down to Cornwall by Parliament to raise the militia on their behalf, but at Launceston the Sheriff proclaimed himself a Royalist, declared the Parliamentary Militia Ordinance invalid, and read the King's Commission of Array. A few days later on 22 August the King raised his standard at Nottingham, and the Civil War began.

Apart from their numerical superiority, the Royalists in Cornwall had two great advantages. One was the command of St Michael's Mount and Pendennis Castle, through which they were able to import arms from France in exchange for tin. The other was the arrival of Sir Ralph Hopton, after being driven west by the Parliamentary forces. A fine professional soldier who had seen service in Germany, he was, like Grenville, a Puritan Royalist, and brought with him a small but invaluable squadron of cavalry. With his dragoons and some three thousand raw militiamen he advanced against Buller, who withdrew from his headquarters at Saltash and took refuge in Plymouth, the great Parliamentary stronghold in the west, and by the end of October Cornwall was in Royalist hands.

Buller died in November, but early in the new year of 1643 Parliament was able to take the offensive. In January the Scottish Colonel Ruthven crossed the Tamar and, advancing through Liskeard, took up a position on the high ground in front of the little church of Bradock. His troops were merely an advance guard, and Hopton, two miles away at Boconnoc, decided to attack before the main body arrived, and on 19

January the battle of Bradock Down, the first on Cornish soil, was fought. It was soon over. Grenville led the foot in so fierce a charge that he broke the enemy line, and the cavalry on the flanks turned defeat into a rout. Parliament's losses were heavy, but it was a merciful victory, for once resistance was over there was no more bloodshed. Ruthven retired on Saltash, but three days later Hopton drove him over the Tamar, again with heavy losses, and once more Cornwall was in Royalist hands.

This little campaign owed its success mainly to the Cornish foot. As the militia were little more than a rabble unwilling to leave their native county, Grenville and the other Royalist gentry organized and trained an army of volunteers, most of them their own servants and tenants, conservative, loyal and bound to their masters by ties of almost feudal devotion. It was the beginning of the famous Cornish infantry that was to make an almost legendary name for itself, and with them Hopton felt confident enough to take the initiative.

In February, therefore, he crossed the Tamar into Devonshire, in an attempt to reduce Plymouth, but he was not yet strong enough, and, driven back on Tavistock, he had to retire into Cornwall. For the moment there was a condition of stalemate, and a short truce was arranged, during which the Royalists recruited and trained their volunteers, and Parliament strengthened the defences of Plymouth. One vitally important outpost was the fort on St Nicholas Island in the Sound, the seaward defence of the town, and of this island and fort Alexander Carew was made governor.

Meanwhile Parliament tried to raise money by an Ordinance sequestrating the estates of those whom it called 'Notorious Delinquents', and appointed county committees to carry out the work. In Cornwall, of course, the Ordinance could not be enforced, though on 27 March a committee was nominated, among the eleven members being Sir Richard Carew, Bart. and Alexander Carew. But Sir Richard was dead.

10

Alexander

The fact that Richard was appointed one of the committee for sequestrating the estates of Cornish Royalists seems to be conclusive proof that he had sided with Parliament. Yet it could be an error. Cornish affairs were still confused, and because Alexander was a Parliamentarian it may have been assumed that so was his father; and that Parliament was not very well informed is evident from their appointing him to another committee for raising money 'for the relief of the Common-wealth' in May, two months after his death. From his writings one gets the impression that whatever Richard may have thought (and everything suggests that he, so proud of being 'descended from the royal race', from kings who were appointed by God, was a confirmed Royalist) he would be too cautious to show his sympathies openly, that he would be one of 'the Third sort', as Clarendon called them, '(for a Party they cannot be call'd) greater than either of the other, both of Fortune, and Number, who, though they were satisfied in their Consciences of the justice of the King's Cause, had yet so great a dread of the Power of the Parliament, that they sat still as Neuters, assisting neither.' After all, Richard was sixty-two when the war began, too old and ill, perhaps, to wish to be involved.

His death is something of a mystery. No will has been found, and although he had written that he had 'reserved a room' for his own body to be laid beside those of his parents in Antony church, there is no record of his having been buried there. But that he was dead by the beginning of April 1643 is proved by the 'Inventory of the goods and Chattells of Sir Richard Carew Barronett of Antony in the Countye of Cornwall deceased. Appraysed . . . the thirteenth daye of Aprill 1643.' First of the three appraisers was Nicholas Skelton ('one of my house', Richard had called him) who on that memorable Whit Sunday had been so stricken on the side of the head as if with two flat stones. Evidently, despite his sartorial eccentricities, Richard dressed expensively, for the first item in the inventory is his 'wearing Appearell', valued at £200 (present value about £3,000). The pity is, we have no portrait of the man who wore these clothes.

His only trophy is this small, grubby piece of paper, for there is no memorial, not even a tablet, in Antony church, to show that he too had lived. Yet Alexander, now Sir Alexander, somehow found time and occasion to pay tribute to his grandfather by adding another inscription to the memorial set up by his father more than twenty years before:

> The verses following were written by Richard Carew of Antony Esq immediately before his death (which happened the Sixth of November 1620) as he was at his private Prayers in his Study (his daily practice) at fower in the afternoon and being found in his Pocket were preserved by his Grandsonne Sr Alexander Carew, according to whose desire they are here set up in memory of him.
>
> Full thirteen fives of years I toyling haue o'repast
> And in the fowerteenth weary, entred am at last. . .
> O by repentance & amendment grant that I
> May still live in thy fear & in thy favour dye.

It is odd that Alexander should have gone to such trouble at this critical time to add a tribute to his grandfather's memorial, and not to have set one up to his father. But if the Civil War had led to an estrangement, his failure to celebrate his father is at least comprehensible.

As he went about his duties on St Nicholas Island there were other things to occupy his thoughts in the spring and summer of 1643. When the truce ended on 22 April, the Parliamentary commander in Devon, Lord Stamford, was ill, and his place was taken by Major-General James Chudleigh, Alexander's cousin, who, although only twenty-five, had distinguished himself on service in Ireland. He lost no time, and on 23 April attacked Hopton's position at Launceston, but was driven back by the arrival of fresh Royalist columns. Hopton pursued him, but was in turn discomfited by a night ambush on Sourton Down, near Okehampton, and retired in some confusion to Launceston.

Among the spoils that Chudleigh took that night was Hopton's despatch-case containing a letter from the King, ordering him to march into Somerset to join the Royalist forces there. Stamford, who had now recovered, resolved to prevent this plan, and, ordering Sir George Chudleigh, James's father, to make a diversion by raiding Bodmin, himself joined young Chudleigh with a force of six thousand men, and took up a strong position on the summit of a hill overlooking Stratton on the upper Tamar. Hopton marched rapidly north and reached Stratton on the evening of the same day, 15 May, and, though short of supplies, decided to attack in the morning, before Sir George Chudleigh could intervene.

The assault began at daybreak, but by three o'clock in the afternoon almost all their powder was spent, and Hopton gave the order to advance without pausing to fire. Led by Grenville and his friends, the infantry pressed on until they reached the top, where Chudleigh led a counter-attack, but by four o'clock the hill was theirs, as were seventeen hundred prisoners, Chudleigh among them. Stamford fled, and reported to Parliament that 'he had been betrayed by James Chudleigh; and that in the heat of the battle, when the hope of the day stood fair, he had voluntarily, with a party, run over to the enemy, and immediately charged the Parliament forces, which begat in all men a general apprehension of treachery, the soldiers fearing their officers', and the officers their soldiers' revolt, and thereupon the rout ensued.' The Royalist version is given by Clarendon in his *History of the Rebellion*. According to this, Stamford spread the report 'to make his own conduct and misfortune the less censured. . . Whereas the truth is, as Chudleigh was a young man of excellent parts and courage, he performed the part of a right good commander, both in his orders and his person; and was taken prisoner in the body of his enemy, whither he had charged with undaunted courage when there was no other expedient in reason left. But this scandal, so without colour cast on him, and entertained with more credit than his services had merited . . . wrought so far upon the young man, together with the kind usage and reception he found as a prisoner among the chief officers, who loved him as a gallant enemy, and one like to do the King good service if he were recovered to his loyalty, that after he had been prisoner about ten days, he freely declared that he was convinced in his conscience and judgment of the errors he had committed; and, upon promise made to him of the King's pardon, frankly offered to join with them in His Majesty's service; and so gave some countenance to the reproach that was first most injuriously cast upon him. The truth is, he was of too good an understanding, and too much generosity in his nature, to be affected to the cause which he served.'

There can be little doubt that Clarendon's account is the true, or approximately true one, but it would be Stamford's version that Alexander received on St Nicholas Island, and, whatever the detail, it soon became clear that his cousin had deserted Parliament's cause for the King's. A few weeks later his uncle, Sir George Chudleigh, followed James's example.

The battle of Stratton was the prelude to one of the most brilliant and romantic campaigns of the war. Having secured Cornwall for the King, Hopton with his three thousand Cornish foot marched through Devonshire into Somerset, where they were joined by Royalist cavalry under Prince Maurice. Occupying Taunton and Bridgwater on the way, by the beginning of July they were at Bath, held for Parliament by Sir William Waller, whose position was at Lansdown, a high Cotswold ridge north of the town. As at Stratton, the Cornish foot stormed the hill, but they were too exhausted to exploit their victory, and their losses were fearful, Grenville being among the dead. Hopton, too, was wounded, and withdrew to Devizes pursued by Waller. There, however, on Roundway

Down, the Royalists, reinforced by cavalry from Oxford, utterly routed their opponents. It was the severest defeat that Parliament had suffered, and opened the way for the seizure of Bristol, after London the most important Parliamentary stronghold in the country.

Bristol fell on 27 July, but again the losses were fearful, particularly those of the Cornishmen, who had been given the task of assaulting the almost impregnable southern defences, and of the army that had left Launceston in May only half remained. Moreover, most of their leaders were gone: Grenville, Sidney Godolphin, and now John Trevanion and Nicholas Slanning, 'both very young, of entire friendship to one another, and to Sir Bevil Grenville'. It was for these men whom they knew, rather than for the abstraction of the King's cause, that the Cornishmen had fought, and now that they were dead, and Hopton left as Governor of Bristol, they refused to follow strangers to besiege Gloucester. There was still a dangerous Parliamentary citadel on the Cornish border, and under Prince Maurice they turned for home.

Although the Cornishmen were no longer the power they had been, either in numbers, discipline or morale, they were credited with almost superhuman qualities, and such was their reputation that, as they marched through the West Country, Parliamentary towns surrendered at their approach—Dorchester, Weymouth, Portland—and by the end of August the great prize of Exeter was about to fall into their hands. And after Exeter it would be the turn of Plymouth, only forty miles away.

There, on St Nicholas Island, Alexander had followed the events of the summer uneasily. Report had it that his cousin and uncle had treacherously deserted the cause of Parliament for that of the King, who had freely pardoned them; and since then the Cornishmen and Cavaliers had won a series of victories that had made the West Country undisputed Royalist territory. Bideford and Barnstaple fell in August, Exeter was falling, and Plymouth, isolated near the end of England, stood alone. Parliament had won no comparable successes elsewhere, and the end of the war seemed imminent, a Royalist victory after the surrender of Plymouth. So Alexander must have brooded on his Island, cut off from the town by half a mile of sea, cut off from his friends, from the distraction and relief of conversation, with little outlet for his energies, little to do but wait for bad news and brood on the impending disaster, the Royalist sequestration of his estates, and the fate of his wife and young children. It was more than flesh and blood, more than Alexander, could stand, and at last his nerve gave way. If his cousin could change sides and be pardoned, so could he. What happened is described by Clarendon:

'Sir Alexander Carew began to think his Island and Fort would hardly secure his estate in Cornwall, and understood the law so well (for he had had a good education) to know that the side he had chosen would be no longer the better than it should continue the stronger; and having originally followed no other motives than of popularity and interest, resolved now to redeem his errors, and found means to correspond with some of his old friends and neighbours in Cornwall, and by them to make a direct overture to surrender that Fort and Island to the King, upon an assurance of His Majesty's pardon, and a full remission of his offences.

'Sir John Berkeley, who then lay before Exeter, was the next supreme officer qualified to entertain such a treaty, and he instantly, by the same conveyance, returned him as ample assurance of his own conditions as could be, with advice that he should not . . . defer the consummating the work, which hereafter, possibly, might not be in his power to effect. . .

'But he was so sottishly and dangerously wary of his own security (having neither courage enough to obey his conscience, nor wickedness enough to be prosperous against it) that he would not proceed till he was sufficiently assured that his pardon was past the Great Seal of England; before which time, though all imaginable haste was made, by the treachery of a servant whom he trusted, his treaty and design was discovered to the Mayor and the rest of the Committee, and according to the diligence used by that party he was suddenly, and without resistance, surprised in his Fort, and carried prisoner into Plymouth.'

It is interesting to compare Clarendon's accounts of the characters and motives of the cousins, James Chudleigh and Alexander Carew. Although it is improbable that Clarendon knew James personally, from what he had heard from Royalist sources it seemed that he was a young man of exceptional courage, intelligence and honour, who in his captivity had learned the truth about the Royalist cause, and changed sides only because he had become convinced that it was the right one. His conversion was the result of genuine conviction; there was nothing dishonourable or treacherous in his conduct, and he had died fighting for the King as loyally as he had formerly fought for Parliament. Clarendon had to admit, however, that the Parliamentary interpretation of the affair was very different from his.

Of Alexander he could speak at first hand, for they had been at Oxford and the Middle Temple together, and were fellow members of the Long Parliament until the outbreak of war. A man without real convictions, his conduct was governed by expediency, not principle, having supported Parliament merely because he thought it would win, and changed his allegiance when the Royalists appeared to be on the point of victory. Moreover, not only did he desert his former friends, but he treacherously tried to betray their defences to their opponents. It is a harsh judgment, but almost certainly a prejudiced one. It is improbable that Alexander, coming from a county that was preponderantly Royalist in sympathy, 'followed no other motives than popularity and interest', and sided with Parliament merely because it was the stronger party. He had been brought up by his father as a Puritan, many of his relations, Chudleighs, Rolles, Strodes, were of the same persuasion, and many of his family's friends and neighbours had been among the principal opponents of the King's despotic rule: John Eliot, John Pym and Francis Rous. Again, Clarendon's charge of cowardice is suspect, for he insinuates that Alexander had a guilty conscience, that he knew in his heart that he should have been with the Royalists. Yet, if he took after his father, we may be sure that he would be 'wary of his own safety', though 'sottishly' is another of the emotional words used by Clarendon to discredit him. ('We have continual need in all our actions, both great and small,' Richard had written, 'to use all the circumspection the foresight of our understanding can reach unto, to avoid any kind of danger, because our duty binds us so to do for our preservation.')

It was 19 August when Alexander was arrested, and soon afterwards he was sent by sea to London. Ironically, his fears proved groundless: Plymouth did not fall to the Royalists, and a few weeks after his arrest, while his cousin James was dying of his wounds, Parliament made an alliance with the Scots, which was completely to change the fortunes of the war. In July 1644 Cromwell and the Scots routed the Royalists at Marston Moor, as a result of which the North was lost to the King, though the West was saved in August, when a Parliamentary army under Essex rashly invaded Cornwall and was forced to surrender at Lostwithiel to the King himself, who directed operations from Boconnoc.

By the end of 1644, however, there could be no doubt that final victory lay with Parliament, and in November, while it was debating the formation of the New Model Army, Alexander was brought to trial on a charge of treason. Although he denied it, a Council of War held at Guildhall found him guilty of 'adhering to the King, and betraying his trust', and condemned him to death. The sentence was delayed, however, for his wife, Jane, by a petition to the House of Commons, pleading his distracted state of mind, gained a reprieve of a month in which he might settle his worldly affairs and prepare for death.

On 20 December he made his will, leaving the custody of his son and heir, John, to his wife, and 'two partes in three of all my lands, tenements and hereditaments' to hold the same 'till that there be raised thereout . . . the full summe of 500^{li} a peece for each of my daughters, and younger children borne and to be borne.' (Evidently Jane was pregnant.) 'And I desire said deare wife to remember her promises concerning my chil-

dren both before our marriage and often since.' On 22
December, a Sunday, he added a codicil in view of 'the violence
of the present warre', making provision for the inability of his
wife or other executors to carry out his will, and leaving two
gold rings of his grandfather to his uncles George and John,
'the one-handed Carew'.

An account of his execution is given in a pamphlet of the
period. 'On Munday, December 23, in the forenoon about 10
of the Clocke, Sir Alexander Carew was brought from the
Tower, guarded by the Lieutenant thereof, and his Officers
(assisted by two companies of the Trained-Bands) unto a
Scaffold erected on Tower Hill for the purpose.' He was only
thirty-five, but much weakened by more than a year's imprisonment and protracted anxiety. At these public spectacles,
however, the assembled multitude expected some edification
from their dying men, but Alexander was anxious only to make
an end, to escape from this public exhibition, and when pressed
by one of the attendant ministers to say something in defence
of his conduct, he cried: 'The greatest enemy against me under
the sun can lay but the suspicion of the fact against me.' And
then we have a glimpse of what he had suffered since his arrest:
'I desire not to spin out time, I desire to be at my period. I have
besought God on my knees oftentimes that I might be dissolved,
and God would never grant it me till now.'

The Lieutenant of the Tower returned to the affair at Plymouth: 'When you went down into Cornwall, these were your
words: You bid me, "God be with you, and I hope I shall give
a good account of my business." '

'I'll lay no blame on any other body, but take all to myself,'
was all that Alexander would say.

As he could not be made to admit his political error, the
minister resumed the spiritual theme: 'We may not desire to go
out of the world but upon a true foundation. The only true
way to salvation is by Christ.'

'I confess it, and I confess my ways, that I am a sinful
creature to God, with all my heart. I thank you all for your
good admonitions; I have surveyed myself over and over again,

with indignation for my sins, and especially my pride. I'll do that duty which I come here for.'

'It is pride that should trouble us all,' the minister prodded him.

But Alexander turned desperately on his tormenting comforters: 'All that you can lay to my charge is but intention, and no man knows my intentions better than myself, and they shall die with myself, put me to what tortures you please. Sir, this is clear, that when I came ashore at Plymouth, I asked them whether they would believe what I said. They told me no. I am in that condition that whatsoever I say is not to be believed, and therefore I have leave to hold my peace.'

As Alexander would say no more, the minister asked whom he would like to stay with him on the scaffold. He had four half-brothers, though the youngest were only boys, and some of them were with him. Turning to them, therefore, he said, 'These are my kindred; my ancestors were counted honest men.' But John, the eldest, was not there. He disowned a brother who had betrayed the cause of Parliament.

His ordeal was not yet over, so far the action had been confined to the stage, but now the groundlings shouted that they wanted to see and hear him, and he was pushed to the front of the scaffold to speak his last words.

'Gentlemen, in consideration of my weak body, I hope you'll not expect that I should speak much to you, neither is it my part nor my desire to discourse of my own actions and to justify myself, but I shall rather confess as the poor Publican did, "Lord, be merciful to me, a sinner." I have desired with unfeigned desire and hearty affection to be dissolved and to be with Christ, knowing it shall be better for me, being assured thereby to be freed from my misery of sin, and enter into a better life. It was the last words and writing of my grandfather, and here of my father, the assurance of their eternal peace and happiness after the dissolution of this body. It is mine likewise. I have no more to say, but I take my humble leave of you.'

The last words of his grandfather were those that he had recently added to his memorial in Antony church:

And yet arriv'd I am not at the port of death,
The port to everlasting Life that openeth.

But apparently he also had with him a copy of his father's
Memoirs, which he held up as he said 'and here of my father'.
It is true that Richard had written them some dozen years
before his death, but almost his last words were: 'When I persuade you to the love, fear and service of our Heavenly Father,
I invite you to the sweetest comfort that ever I had, which
makes me desirous even of that dissolution which so affrights
and astonishes the hearts of all carnal men, that they loathe and
abhor the very name of death; yet, I praise my God, it is more
precious unto me than was my birth, because it will be the
beginning of my new and everlasting life.' Whatever discord
there may have been between father and son when the war
began, it had been resolved in prison, and Alexander's tribute
on the scaffold is Richard's true memorial.

Alexander then asked them all to join in the twenty-third
Psalm, 'The Lord is my shepherd,' the singing of which he
himself led. When it was finished, the executioner asked his
pardon for what he was about to do, and giving him money, he
said, 'I forgive thee, and thank thee too. Prithee leave my
clothes, take my head, and do it handsomely.' Then, bidding
his friends 'God be with you,' he turned again to the executioner: 'Dost thou hear; when I say "Lord, though Thou
killest me, yet will I put my trust in Thee," then do thou cut off
my head, for it was the last words that ever my mother spoke
when she died.'

And when he had said, 'Lord, into Thy hands I commend
my spirit,' he laid himself down with his head over the block,
and as he spoke his mother's last words the executioner did his
office.

His body was buried in the Church of St Augustine,
Hackney.

It was a wretched, though not ignoble end, and one cannot
help wondering how far his upbringing was responsible for his
fate. Deprived of his mother before he was two, during the
most impressionable years of his life he was subjected to his

father's constant admonitions and exhortations, taught that the eye of God was constantly upon him, the Devil always lying in wait for his soul to feed the fires of Hell, that even the most carefree diversion was fraught with a solemn moral. The intense, emotionally overcharged atmosphere of his father's house may well have sapped the vitality and character of an only son, adored, and probably spoiled. Clarendon accused him of weakness, and was probably right, yet he suffered an intolerable strain during that fatal summer of 1643. If he really intended to surrender St Nicholas Island to the Royalists, not merely, like his cousin, to change his allegiance, his treachery was unpardonable, yet he maintained to the end that he was condemned on suspicion only, that all that he could be charged with was intention.

There is a story still current at Antony House, that when Alexander sided with Parliament 'his family' cut his portrait out of its frame, and that when he tried to join the King they replaced it. Such traditions often have an element of truth, and if Richard, despite his Puritanism, remained a Royalist, he may well have thus symbolically dissociated himself from his son's action. He could not have replaced it, however, for he died five months before Alexander's change of sides. Yet, whoever was responsible, the canvas has certainly been cut at top and bottom, and stitched together again.

11

John

In June 1645 the New Model Army routed the Royalists at Naseby, and a few weeks later Fairfax and Cromwell were in the West Country, where their victory at Langport and capture of Bridgwater virtually ended the war. Under Hopton, however, Cornwall held out until the following March, although even then Sir John Arundell refused to surrender Pendennis Castle to Fairfax. He remembered the treachery of his great-nephew, Alexander, and wrote:

> Sir, the Castle was committed to my government by His Majesty, who by our laws hath the command of the Castles and Forts of this Kingdom, and my age of seventy summons me hence shortly. Yet I shall desire no other testimony to follow my departure than my conscience to God and loyalty to His Majesty, whereto I am bound by all the obligations of nature, duty and oath. I wonder you demand the Castle without Authority from His Majesty, which if I should render, I brand myself and my posterity with the indelible character of Treason. And having taken less than two minutes resolution, I resolve that I will here bury myself before I deliver up this Castle to such as fight against His Majesty, and that nothing you can threaten is formidable to me in respect of the loss of loyalty and conscience. Your servant, John Arundell of Trerice, 16th March, 1646.

It was August before he capitulated, unable any longer to endure the slow starvation of women, children and wounded in his charge, and on 17 March 'Jack for the King' and his garrison marched out with their horses and arms, 'colours flying, trumpets sounding, drums beating, matches lighted at both ends, and bullets in their mouths'. In Cornwall, the Civil War ended as heroically as it had begun.

There was no reason why he should have resisted longer. In May the King had given himself up to the Scots, but after fruitless negotiations they handed him over to Parliament, who confined him in Holdenby House. One of the commissioners appointed to receive him was John Carew.

At this time, the beginning of 1647, John was just twenty-four. More fortunate than Alexander in having had a mother to bring him up, and three brothers to compete with, he was a far stronger character. After Oxford he had entered the Inner Temple, where he was a contemporary of Edmund Ludlow, another staunch Parliamentarian who had seen much service in the war. In February 1647 he entered Parliament as member for Tregony, and in the following year served as a County Commissioner of Militia in Cornwall. Could it have been he who slashed Alexander's portrait out of its frame? He was quite capable of doing so, and Alexander's widow, Lady Jane, and her fourteen-year-old son, Sir John, would have been unable to prevent him. To his father's courage, obstinancy and puritanical devoutness, John added a political and religious fanaticism that made him, young as he was, a formidable opponent, as the King was to find, for in January 1649 he was appointed a Judge of the High Court of Justice erected by the Commons to try 'Charles Stewart, King of England'. John was one of those who signed his death warrant.

After the execution of the King, although the exiled Royalists proclaimed his son as Charles II, England was a republic governed by a Council of State and the 'Rump', all that remained of the House of Commons, the Lords having been abolished. This was much to the liking of John and other Fifth Monarchy Men, who believed that the republic was, after the fall of the empires of Assyria, Persia, Greece and Rome, the prelude to a fifth, the Kingdom of Christ and his Saints, who were to rule for a thousand years.

In 1651 John became a member of the Council of State, and it would be pleasant to think that in the following year he was sufficiently of this world to be interested in a pamphlet in John Bartlet's shop, the Gilt Cup, in St Paul's Churchyard:

Excellent Helps really found out, tried, and had, whereof the parties hereafter mentioned are true and sufficient witnesses, by a Warming-stone in his case, which not costing much, will save much cost in fire, and withal avoid the danger of fire. And likewise is very useful and comfortable for the colds of aged and sick people, and for women with child or in childbed, and for sucking and young children, and such as have their hearing and seeing decaying, and for the toothache, sore throats, and the cold fits of agues. As also for fluxes, rheums, collics, ruptures, and many other infirmities, or any cold diseases, and for those that in beds, studies, shops, ships, churches or elsewhere have need of heat, yet cannot conveniently make use of fire. And likewise for the poor, when having no fire of their own, they may borrow the heating of this stone at a neighbour's fire, if his charity be not altogether cold.

Published by Sir Richard Carew, Baronet, for the honour of God, from whom every good gift comes, and for the good of all people, from the new-born babe to the decrepit and decaying old man. Printed for John Bartlet, 1652.

It was twelve years since Bartlet had received Richard's manuscript, shortly before the outbreak of the war, during which people had more urgent things to think about than warming-stones, but now in the more settled time of the Republic he had laid in a stock of Polyphant stones, complete with cases. 'They give not only a greater, but a sweeter heat than Warming-Pans,' he added, and, 'Keep the case dry, or it will sweat.' Bartlet had little to learn about the arts of advertising and salesmanship, though he did not know that the inventor had been dead nine years.

All was not well, however, with the new Republic. Parliament and the Army were at loggerheads. In April 1653 Cromwell expelled the Rump, and by the end of the year he was Protector of the Commonwealth of the British Isles and its colonies. For Fifth Monarchy Men this was a blasphemous betrayal of the coming Kingdom of Christ, and early in 1654, in *The Grand Catastrophe or the Change of Government*, 'Johannes Cornubiensis', almost certainly John Carew, protested, 'There are those who suspect you'll *King* it, and procure your *Heir* to succeed you.' A number of Fifth Monarchy Men were imprisoned, and John formed one of a deputation of four who went to Cromwell to demand the release of these 'Prisoners of the Lord'. The Protector assured them that if they really were prisoners of the Lord they would soon be set at liberty, for nobody in England was 'a prisoner for the Lord's sake or the Gospel'. This was not an answer to placate fanatics, and when the four men refused to appear before the Council, they were arrested and brought to trial. They were uncompromising, and John roundly declared that Cromwell had 'taken the Crown off from the head of Christ and put it upon his own.' As a result he spent the next two years as a prisoner in Pendennis Castle, the scene of his great-uncle's heroic defence ten years before.

Cromwell died in 1658, and was succeeded, as John had foreseen, by his son Richard. But the new Protector was not made of the same mettle as his father, and when the Rump, which included John, was restored in 1659, it abolished the Protectorate. The end of the Republic was also in sight, and after a confused struggle for power the House of Stuart was restored to the throne, and in May 1660 Charles II landed at Dover.

It was a restoration not only of a King but also of the Royalist gentry, and though Clarendon, as Charles's principal minister, tried to prevent vindictive acts of vengeance against their fallen opponents, the new Parliament ordered Cromwell's body to be exhumed, hanged at Tyburn and buried at the gallow's foot. Nor did the Commons, still less the restored House of Lords, intend to let those who had been responsible for the execution of Charles I go unpunished, and the regicides were ordered to give themselves up within fourteen days. Some of them, like Edmund Ludlow, escaped abroad, but John Carew at once obeyed the summons. He was, perhaps, eager, even over-eager, to be a martyr, for in *Revelations* 20. 4 it was written: 'And I saw the souls of them that were beheaded for the witness of Jesus, and for the word of God, and which had not worshipped the beast . . . and they lived and reigned with Christ a thousand years.'

John was in Cornwall when he heard of the order to surrender, and although his friends urged him to escape, which would have been easy, he refused, saying, 'that he had committed both his life and estate to the Lord, to save or destroy, as he thought meet; and therefore he would not by any means go out of the way,' and at once set off for London. At Looe he was arrested, but when the officer, whose warrant was for John Cary, found that his name was Carew, he would have let him go, had not John assured him that he really was the man he wanted.

According to a sympathetic Puritan account, 'After he was seized upon in the Countrey, and coming up to London, he had a gratious presence of the Lord with him . . . otherwise the many reproaches and hard usage in the way had been sufficient to have troubled his spirit. In most Towns where he came, the Generality of the people Reviling him with such words as these: hang him Rogue, pistol him, said others, hang him up said some (at Salisbury) at the next sign-post without any further trouble. Look, said others, how he doth not alter his Countenance, but we believe he will tremble when he comes to the Ladder. This is the rogue will have no King but Jesus. Indeed, the rage of the people all the way was such, that had he not been indued with strength from on High, he could not have under-gone the wicked and Barbarous Deportment and Carriage of the Giddy multitude.'

In his *Memoirs*, written in exile, Ludlow describes John's trial on 11 October: how he was continually interrupted and denied Counsel, so that 'when he saw that all he could say was to no purpose, he frankly acknowledged that he had sat in the High Court of Justice, and had signed two Warrants, one for summoning the Court in order to the King's Tryal, and another for his Execution,' adding, however, that he had acted under the authority of Parliament. As he was rarely allowed to finish anything that he tried to speak in his own defence, and as at least one of his judges gave evidence against him as a witness, he turned to the jury, 'appealing to their Consciences, whether he had been permitted to make his Defence. But they, who were not to be diverted from the Resolutions they had taken, without any regard to the manner of his Tryal, declared him Guilty.' Although Ludlow's is a partisan account, it is probably essentially true, though it is only fair to quote a Royalist comment: 'It is no wonder that he was one of the Judges of the King, who was consenting unto the death of his own Brother.'

Like Major-General Harrison, another leading regicide and Fifth Monarchy Man, John was condemned to be hanged, drawn and quartered: that is, to be strangled until half dead, cut down, disembowelled and hacked into four pieces. In spite of this appalling prospect, all the time he was in prison 'his joy in the Lord was such, that when many came drooping in spirit so him (by reason of the Gloominesse of this present dispensation) they went away refreshed and comforted by those many Gracious words that came out of his mouth.' Convinced that he was right, he assured them that he believed in the resurrection of his cause 'as much as he did that his body should rise again, and if he did not believe that he should not be so cheerful.'

When, on 13 October, he was told that Harrison had been executed, 'cut down alive, and saw his Bowels thrown into the fire,' he merely remarked, 'Well, my turn will be next.' The following day was a Sunday, and that night he was visited by 'some of his Natural Relations', no doubt his brothers, who wept when they took leave of him. They told him that his nephew and some others were doing their utmost for his reprieve, but he replied, 'There is nothing to be done: For the Sheriffe hath brought me word (just now) that I must Dye tomorrow, and that there was some desired I might not be Quartered, but it would not be granted.' If, as one hopes, the nephew were Alexander's son, Sir John, who was one of the members for the county in this Convention Parliament, he was acting with uncommon magnanimity in trying to save the man who had been 'consenting to the death' of his own father.

The next morning, as John 'was coming down Newgate stairs to go into the Sledge, in a very smiling, cheerful manner, his countenance shining with great glory, he uttered words to this effect: "My Lord Jesus endured the Crosse, whose steps I desire to follow." The cheerfulness of his countenance all the way as he went to the Gibbet, remained.' That is the Puritan version, but unhappily his enemies had another and crueller interpretation: 'And on Monday following, he was drawn from Newgate to Charing Cross on a Hurdle; First having prepared himself by drinking three pintes of Sack to bear up his spirits, which caused a more than ordinary flushing in his face all the way he went, and sweat so much, that his Handkerchief could scarcely keep the water from running down his face.'

Alexander had had little to say before his execution, but, like his father, the more John spoke the more he had to say, and after twenty minutes of his speech from the scaffold the crowd began to grow restive, and, 'Mr Sheriffe interrupted him, saying, " 'Tis desired that you spend the rest of your time in preparing your selfe." Another said, "You spend your self, Sir, in this discourse." Another said, "It raines." Then Mr Carew said, "I will pray." ' It reads like the tragic prose of Hemingway.

So long was John's prayer that he had to pause before he could finish: ' "I am so exceeding Dry that my tongue is ready to stick to my Mouth. But I would fain speak a little more. . ." A friend that stood by said, "It is expected you should speak something to the matter of your suffering." The Under-Sheriffe said, " 'Tis not to be suffered. What are you that you put on men to speak? What are you, Sir?" '

But John, now on the ladder with the halter round his neck, turned to the executioner: ' "Stay a while, I will speak one word." And then said very solemnly and with a loud voyce, "Lord Jesus, receive my Soul. Lord Jesus, into thy Armes I Commend my Spirit." And so fell Asleep.'

With a brutal briskness, the Royalist report concludes: 'Being turned off the Ladder, he was soon dead and quartered.' His bowels were burned, and his head and quarters dragged naked through the streets back to Newgate. One of his brothers begged them of the King, and by him they were obscurely buried.

A hundred years before, in 1560 at the beginning of Queen Elizabeth's reign, the first Richard Carew was a boy of five. Since that time England had fought a twenty years' war with Spain and suffered another twenty years of political upheaval; the Armada had been defeated and a king executed. Three generations had lived and died. And now, at Antony in Cornwall, Alexander's son, Sir John, a young man of twenty-six, took up the threads of life again, and perhaps forgetting the past, had his father's name and baronet's helm added to his portrait, and restored it to its frame.

APPENDIX I

The Carews of Antony and the Edgcumbes

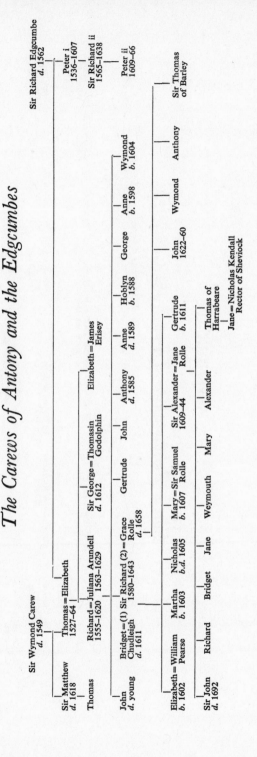

APPENDIX II

Carew Relationships Through the Chudleighs

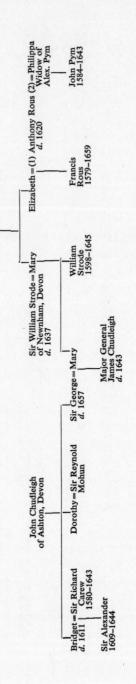

Bibliography

Antony House MSS
The Booke of M^as Richard Carew (1628–30). CZ/EE/32
Sir Richard Carewes Booke (1637). CZ/EE/32
Carew-Chudleigh Marriage Settlement, 1601. CS/II/5
Portwrickle Quay Agreement, 1612. CD/AJ/1
Will of Richard Carew i, 1620. CW/GG/5
Carew-Rolle Marriage Settlement, 1621 CS/II/11
Carew-Rolle Marriage Settlement, 1633. CS/II/16
Baronetcy Patent, 1641. CO/Q/22
Inventory of Goods of Sir Richard Carew, 1643. CW/GG/35

Excellent Helps . . . by a Warming-stone. Published by Sir Richard Carew, 1652.
The True and Readie Way to Learne the Latin Tongue. Attested by . . . Mr Richard Carew, 1654.
The Voice of the Lord in the Temple, 1640.

Coate, Mary. *Cornwall in the Great Civil War and Interregnum*, 1933, 2nd ed. 1963. (The author confuses Sir Richard Carew with his father, the first Richard.)
Donald, M. B. *Burchard Kranich, Miner and Queen's Physician.* Annals of Science, Vol. 6, No. 3, Vol. 7, No. 1.
Halliday, F. E. *Richard Carew of Antony*, 1953.
Hull, P. L. *Richard Carew's Discourse about the Duchy Suit.* Journal of the Royal Institution of Cornwall, 1962.
Rowse, A. L. *Tudor Cornwall*, 1941.
Turnbull, G. H. *Hartlib, Dury and Comenius*, 1947.

Bate, George. *The Lives . . . of the Principall Contrivers of that Horrid Murder of . . . King Charles I*, 1661.

Commons Journals, 1625–1660.

Clarendon, Earl of. *The History of the Rebellion and Civil Wars in England*, 1702–4.

'Cornubiensis, Johannes.' *The Grand Catastrophe or the Change of Government*, 1654.

Heath, James. *A Brief Chronicle of the Late Intestine War*, 1663.

Ludlow, Lieutenant-General Edmund. *Memoirs*, 1699.

Noble, Mark. *The Lives of the English Regicides*, 1798.

The Speech or Confession of Sir Alexander Carew, Baronet, 1644.

The Speeches and Prayers of some of the late King's Judges, 1660.

Index

Antony Church, 70, 94, 133–5, 136, 145
Antony House, 16, 63, 96, 108, 120
Archery, 55
Armada, 18, 37
Arundell, John i, 17
Arundell, John ii, 18, 45, 54, 141, 142, 156
Arundell (Carew), Juliana, 18, 72
Atwell, Hugh, 63

Bache, Mr, 133–4
Bacon, Sir Francis, 98
Bartlet, John, 135, 139, 157
Bligh, William, 111–13
Boconnoc, 15, 45, 59, 142, 151
Booke of Mas Richard Carew, The, 105–22, 154
Bradock Down, battle, 143
Bristol, 148
Bubb, Captain, 115
Buckingham, Duke of, 98, 101, 102
Buller, Sir Richard, 142
Burcot, Dr (Burchard Cranach), 84–90
Burghley, Lord, 24–33, 88–90

Camden, William, 19, 61

Carew, Alexander, 63, 73, 104, 124, 138, 142–55;
portrait, 120, 155, 157, 163
Carew (Pearse), Elizabeth, 52, 100, 133
Carew, Sir Francis, 79
Carew, Sir George, 19, 41, 54, 55, 73
Carew, Gertrude, 63, 70, 75
Carew, John i, 35, 44, 76, 93, 152
Carew, John ii, 100, 153, 157–62
Carew, John iii, 124, 141, 151, 157, 163
Carew, Martha, 52, 72
Carew, Mary, 59
Carew, Nicholas, 58–9
Carew, Richard i, birth, 17; marriage, 18; Duchy Suit, 23–33; blindness, 82–4; death, 93; 145
Carew, Richard ii, birth, 18; childhood, 34–8; Oxford, 38; Middle Temple, 38; travels, 41–4; marriage, 44; recreations, 47–51, 139; M.P., 78, 97; remarriage, 100; writings, 102–22, 124–31, 139; baronetcy, 140; death, 143
Carew, Wymond, 57
Carnsew, Sir Richard, 84

Carnsew, William i, 17, 84, 86
Carnsew, William ii, 17, 54, 68, 93
Chark, 66
Charles I, 101, 123, 131, 133, 151, 157
Charles II, 157, 159
Chudleigh (Carew), Bridget, 44, 46–60, 69–71, 154
Chudleigh (Mohun), Dorothy, 45, 59
Chudleigh, Sir George, 146–7
Chudleigh, Major-General James, 145–7
Civil War, 142–56
Clarendon, Earl of, 139, 144, 146, 149–51
Clyes, Rawe, 65–7
Cotehele, 16
Cotton, Sir Robert, 63
Courtenay, Peter, 116
Cromwell, Oliver, 158–9
Cundy, John, 116–17

Edgcumbe, Peter i, 54, 84, 86
Edgcumbe, Sir Richard i, 16
Edgcumbe, Sir Richard ii, 84
Eliot, Sir John, 35, 78, 101, 102
Elizabeth I, 28, 52, 86–90
Essex, Earl of, 24, 27, 28, 38
Examination of Men's Wits, The, 19–20
Excellency of the English Tongue, The, 61–2
Excellent Helps by a Warming-Stone, 135, 158
Exeter, 24, 148

Fairfax, Edward, 21
Feats, 89–92
Fifth Monarchy Men, 157–61
Fitzgeoffrey, Charles, 44
Fortescue, Edmond, 84, 91

Frobisher, 111–13
Fuller, Thomas, 97

Godfrey of Bulloigne, 21–2
Godolphin, Sir Francis, 19, 26, 54
Gorges, Sir Ferdinando, 59–61
Grand Catastrophe, The, 158
Greenwich Palace, 26, 29
Grenville, Sir Bevil, 137, 138, 141, 142, 143, 146–7

Halton, 35
Harrison, Major-General, 161
Hartlib, Samuel, 139
Herring's Tail, A, 39–40
Hopton, Sir Ralph, 142, 146–8
Howard, Lord of Effingham, 28
Hunsdon, Lord, 86

James I, 55, 78, 79, 98

Killigrew, Sir Henry, 26, 31
Killigrew, William, 24, 26, 27, 28, 29

Lanhydrock, 15, 98
Lansdown, battle, 147
Laud, Archbishop, 102, 123, 131, 133, 137
Lobb, Joan, 113–14
Ludlow, Edmund, 157, 159, 160

Maynard, Mr, 31, 99
Mohun, Sir Reynold, 45, 54
Mohun, Sir William, 86
Mount Edgcumbe, 16

Nance, John, 30
Nashe, Thomas, 39
Neville, Sir Henry, 41
Norden, John, 62

Peele, George, 90
Pendennis Castle, 42, 142, 156, 159
Periam, Sir William, 31
Plymouth, 142, 143, 148
Plymouth Company, 60
Port Eliot, 78
Portwrinkle, 79–82
Precious water, 72–3, 100
Prynne, William, 131
Pym, John, 35, 38, 45, 101–2, 137–8, 141

Raleigh, Sir Walter, 24, 25, 38, 54
Rolle (Carew), Grace, 100
Rolle (Carew), Jane, 124, 151, 157
Roundway Down, battle, 148
Rous, Anthony, 35, 54
Rous, Francis, 35, 38, 45, 101, 139

St Germans, 35, 78, 101
St Nicholas Island, 143, 148–9
Shakespeare, William, 26, 61
Sherborne, 25

Sheviock, 79
Shillingham, 16, 142
Sidney, Sir Philip, 17, 18, 62
Sir Richard Carewes Booke, 124–31
Skelton, Nicholas, 134, 145
Sourton Down, battle, 146
Southcote, Thomas, 48
Stamford, Lord, 145–6
Strafford, Earl of, 123, 133, 137, 138
Stratton, battle, 146
Strode, Sir William, 45
Survey of Cornwall, The, 19, 37, 44, 51–5, 57, 62, 63, 65

Theobalds, 31
Trelawny, Jonathan, 23, 30
Trerice, 17, 18, 128

Voice of the Lord in the Temple, The, 133–5

Warming-stone, 52, 126, 135, 158
Warwick, Countess of, 28
Wood, Anthony, 48